Differentiating Language Arts Instruction for Students With Special Needs in Inclusive Settings, Grades K–5

Differentiating Language Arts Instruction for Students With Special Needs in Inclusive Settings, Grades K–5

Howard G. Sanford

Donald S. Marozas

Erin Lane Marozas

James R. Patton

pro·ed
An International Publisher

8700 Shoal Creek Boulevard
Austin, Texas 78757
800/897-3202 Fax 800/397-7633
www.proedinc.com

© 2011 by PRO-ED, Inc.
8700 Shoal Creek Boulevard
Austin, Texas 78757-6897
800/897-3202   Fax 800/397-7633
www.proedinc.com

Library of Congress Cataloging-in-Publication Data

Differentiating language arts instruction for students with special needs in inclusive
settings, grades K-5 / Howard G. Sanford ... [et al.].
      p. cm.
   Includes bibliographical references.
   ISBN 978-1-4164-0467-5
   1. Special education—United States. 2. Reading (Elementary)—United States. 3.
Individualized reading instruction—United States. 4. Language arts (Elementary)—United
States. I. Sanford, Howard G.
   LB3973.5.D55 2010
   371.9'0446—dc22
                                                                        2009053057

Art Director: Jason Crosier
Designer: Susan TeVrucht
This book is designed in Agenda and Minion.

Printed in the United States of America

1 2 3 4 5 6 7 8 9 10   19 18 17 16 15 14 13 12 11 10

CONTENTS

ACKNOWLEDGMENTS

We would like to thank the many professional colleagues, former graduate and undergraduate students, and teachers in the field of special and general education who have supported our lengthy commitment to this project. We are grateful to Betty and Jim Lane, whose proofreading skills and reality checks regarding what teachers need and are looking for in a book proved most helpful. Special thanks must go to Margaret Sanford for her support and patience.

We would also like to thank Kathy Synatschk, Executive Editor at PRO-ED, for her guidance—from the initial conceptualization of the book to its ultimate completion. The help and guidance of PRO-ED Editor Chris Anne Worsham has been invaluable, as were the specific suggestions and support provided by PRO-ED Production Editor Melissa Tullos. We are most grateful to Dawn Rowe, whose secretarial skills are second to none. Her unselfish, generous gift of time and sacrifice is a much sought-after commodity in today's busy world.

INTRODUCTION

Today's general education teacher faces many challenges in the school. In addition to cutbacks in budgets and an increasing amount of required paperwork, teachers are having to address the education and personal needs of a wide range of students. These students require teachers to possess a teaching skill set quite different from that of years past (Hoover & Patton, 2008). This resource is a practical guide that will assist teachers in addressing the academic performance of students with differing needs—especially students with disabilities—in language arts. The specific language arts skill areas covered in this guide are reading, written expression, and oral language (listening, speaking).

In the early days of special education, many students with disabilities were removed from general education classrooms, instead receiving their education in a self-contained—and typically, a physically segregated—setting. The teachers of these students usually developed and taught a functional, life skills–oriented curriculum. Concurrently, students in general education classes (Grades K–5) received an academically oriented curriculum.

As the trend toward increased inclusion of students with disabilities into general education classrooms has continued, more students with disabilities are receiving their education in general education settings. Consequently, the instructional pressure on all teachers to teach increasingly complex curricula (special education and general education) while addressing a wide array of needs became greater. Meeting the demands of increased educational quality and accountability (America 2000, No Child Left Behind, 2001) for all students, while simultaneously attempting to meet the special education/related service and transition service requirements of the Individuals with Disabilities Education Act (IDEA, 1997), and its most recent reauthorization, the Individuals with Disabilities Education Improvement Act (IDEIA, 2004), created many challenges for teachers.

An examination of the academic learning standards content developed by the three states with the largest school populations (California, Texas, and New York; see Note) revealed that these states focus on the same general academic areas: English/language arts (ELA), mathematics, and science and social studies. Furthermore, they require formal academic achievement testing in these four areas, beginning at the elementary level (Grades 3 and 4) and continuing with similar testing at the middle and high school levels. All students with disabilities are required to participate in these state tests through one of two general options:

1. complete the specific required academic tests at the various grade levels with or without appropriate and approved accommodations, or
2. complete approved alternative assessments based on Individualized Education Program (IEP) content.

Historically, many students with various learning and behavioral disabilities have not flourished within the traditional large-group instructional format that is frequently used in general education classrooms; however, it is in general education classrooms that these students receive most of their academic instruction in contemporary schools. Many students with disabilities have the potential to pass the mandated examinations within specific areas of the language arts curriculum if instruction is adjusted to better meet their individual learning needs. This goal can be addressed with the implementation of appropriate instructional adaptations and the infusion of real-life content within academic activities.

All students need preparation for the demands of adulthood. For some students with disabilities, real-life skills content will be emphasized in their IEPs and is critical to achieving independent functioning later in life. Without a solid, functional skills–based curriculum, many students would be ill prepared for dealing effectively with the varied demands of adulthood (Blalock, Patton, Kohler, & Bassett, 2008). We believe a curriculum that is organized so as to integrate academic content at each grade level with life skills topics (career/work related, home and family, leisure time, community living, and emotional and physical health) would achieve three goals:

1. covering essential academic content,
2. preparing students to take and succeed on required state tests, and
3. providing coverage of critical real-life skills.

We suggest that schools work toward infusing and integrating life skills content within existing language arts academic content. Students without disabilities will benefit from exposure to higher academic standards combined with opportunities to use academic skills within a life skills framework. Students with disabilities will be a part of the academic focus of the classroom while still receiving instruction in functional areas. For a classroom to be truly inclusionary (not just sharing the same physical space), teaching all students similar skills or content at the same time is certainly desirable. However, few curricular resources exist that specifically address inclusionary academic activities for use in general education classrooms. We thus developed *Differentiating Language Arts Instruction* as a resource for classroom teachers at the K–5 grade levels to assist them in teaching English/language arts content to students with disabilities. This text offers a number of instructional outlines in the specific skill areas of reading (word identification, comprehension), written expression (prewriting, writing, postwriting), and oral language (listening, speaking).

Appropriate *instructional inclusion*, sometimes referred to as *responsible inclusion*, versus mere physical inclusion should mean that students with disabilities will be able to participate in a variety of activities through the use of appropriate strategies and supports. If successfully implemented, these strategies and supports will allow many students with disabilities to truly participate in the instructional curriculum offered in general education programs and will also have a greater potential for academic success on state-mandated ELA tests.

The instructional information in this book is offered in the form of instructional outlines. Each outline offers teaching ideas that focus on specific skill areas related to ELA, as well as a matching set of specific and varied techniques to provide appropriate instructional differentiation for students with disabilities. In addition, each outline includes a variety of instructional suggestions for the infusion, integration, generalization, and transfer of real-life skills. These areas of real-life content are embedded within a model, Demands of Adulthood, suggested by Cronin,

Patton, and Wood (2007) and Patton, Cronin, and Wood (1999). The result is more than 500 specific suggestions for integrating real-life content with language arts skill areas.

Instructional Outline Tables

In *Differentiating Language Arts Instruction,* the instructional outlines contain tables that provide hundreds of practical ideas and suggestions for teaching activities that special education teachers who are serving as collaborative teachers within inclusive classrooms can use. Information in the tables can be used to develop interventions and activities to better equip and enable students to succeed within the language arts curriculum. These tables provide a mechanism whereby general education teachers and special education personnel can truly work together to deliver effective instruction to students with disabilities who are in inclusive language arts classrooms.

There are 90 instructional outlines: 42 for reading, 36 for written expression, and 12 for oral language. Each outline contains four suggested activities, with matching instructional differentiation activities, to teach the identified skill.

For instance, a second-grade teacher can find several activities to teach prediction, compound words, or editing mechanics; each activity includes suggestions for differentiating the activity to better meet the needs of students with disabilities. The recommended differentiating ideas are appropriate for students with a range of needs. These activities can be further adapted to reflect instructional changes that have been suggested or documented as successful for students within the ELA-related content of student IEPs or Section 504 plans. Teachers can use the suggested activities to (a) generate instructional activities or specific lesson plans that match a local district's needs or (b) address specific skills and objectives based on that state's priority ELA standards. The goal is to enable children with special needs to participate in the same lesson on the same topic at the same time as their peers who are not disabled.

Differentiated instruction is actually a reapplication of individualized instruction that enables teachers to accommodate a wide range of student needs within the academic curricula required for general education classrooms. Hall (2002) stated,

> Differentiated instruction is a process to approach teaching and learning for students of differing abilities in the same class. The intent of differentiating instruction is to maximize each student's growth and individual success by meeting each student where he or she is, and assisting the learning process. (p. 2)

The examples of differentiated instruction provided in each outline for each area of language arts within this guide offer teachers a variety of suggestions for specific instructional alterations that they can provide within general education classrooms. These teacher-directed instructional alterations can extend from the "what" of instruction (e.g., cutting back on the specific scope of what particular students will learn, providing alternative topics for students to learn, substituting a particular real-life situation topic for the examples provided in the class textual material) to the "how" of instruction. For example, an individual student may learn a particular language arts skill through the use of different materials, product outcomes, or types of student assistance (e.g., peers, technology).

Each instructional outline also contains six recommendations for integrating real-life skills into the academic content that is being covered. These real-life skills suggestions are organized according to five domains (Career Awareness/Work Related, Home and Family, Leisure Time, Community Living, Emotional/Physical Health), as conceptualized by Cronin et al. (2007). Teachers thus have a resource to help ensure the inclusion of real-life curricular content that might address a primary IEP component for specific students with disabilities. The infusion of real-life-skills content within academic content is a useful instructional tool and typically leads to more motivation and enhanced learning opportunities for all students in an inclusive classroom (Cronin et al., 2007; Patton et al., 1999). Moreover, because the approximately 500 life-skills-content activities contained in the tables are directly related to specific ELA skills, these activities can serve as an excellent resource/referent for the development of alternative assessments required by IDEA 1997 and IDEIA 2004 (Taylor, 2009; Thompson & Thurlow, 2001; Ysseldyke & Olsen, 1999).

Note

Based on a review of California's K–12 Academic Content Standards, New York's State Learning Standards, and the Texas Essential Knowledge and Skills (TEKS).

READING

Word Study

>	Phonics and Structural Analysis
>	Sight Word and Vocabulary Development
>	Context Clues and Reference Sources

Reading Comprehension

>	Predicting/Drawing Conclusions/Making Inferences
>	Main Idea
>	Classifying and Categorizing
>	Cause and Effect

Introduction

The importance of reading and its relationship to academic success in all subject areas at all grade levels, as well as its connection to career success and personal independence, have been well established. In addition, problems with reading acquisition and/or continued failure in reading for students who exhibit special needs, particularly students with learning disabilities (Hammill & Bartel, 2004; Wiederholt & Bryant, 2001), is a major challenge facing classroom teachers. An analysis of commercial reading programs, district- and state-wide reading standards, and required state and national examinations in reading has identified a generic core of word identification skill areas, which includes sight words, vocabulary development, phonics and structural analysis, and the use of context clues and reference sources. In addition, a number of educators have historically supported the premise that reading comprehension is the most critical school-based academic skill due to the fact that the overall goal of reading is for students to gain meaning from the printed word (Carnine, Silbert, Kame'enui, & Tarver, 2004; Gray, 1940; Hammill, 2004; Hammill & Bartel, 2004; Mastropieri & Scruggs, 1997; RAND Reading Study Group, 2002). Three skill areas related to word study and four skill areas related to overall reading comprehension have been emphasized throughout the research literature, commercial programs, and state academic standards:

1. main idea,
2. classification and categorization,
3. cause and effect, and
4. predicting, drawing conclusions, and making inferences.

This section of this resource for teachers offers suggested activities to teach each of these word identification and comprehension skill areas through a variety of class and large-group activities, instructional differentiation suggestions for individuals and small groups, and related examples of integrated real-life activities.

Phonics and Structural Analysis

Classroom Activities

A. Children will make a letter book by illustrating each page with something that starts with the given letter.

B. After reading a poem on a chart, children will circle each occurrence of the target letter.

C. From a group of 8 to 10 objects, the student will identify the objects that begin with the target letter.

D. The class will play "I Spy" using a "something that starts with . . . ." format. Children will take turns guessing.

Differentiated Instruction

→ Children will make a class letter book by finding a magazine picture of something that starts with the given letter.

→ When shown words containing the target letter and some words without the target letter, children will say yes if it has the target letter in it or no if it does not have it.

→ From a group of 8 to 10 <u>labeled</u> objects, the student will identify the objects that begin with the target letter.

→ The class will play "I Spy." The format will be "I spy with my little eye things that start with . . . ." Each child will have a picture (or actual object) and will hold up his or her picture when his or her letter is named.

Integration of Real-Life Topics

- **Career Awareness/Work Related**
  Children will state their parents' job titles and tell the letter/sound with which they start.

- **Home and Family**
  When feeding the family pets, or during a family discussion of a story, video, or photo about pets, children will recognize which bowl belongs to which animal by its name on the bowl.

- **Leisure Time**
  Children will complete a puzzle of objects that begin/ end with a letter currently being learned.

- **Community Living**
  Children will collect items from their community that begin with the target letter (i.e., when the class is learning about "L," they all collect leaves).

- **Emotional/Physical Health**
  Children will sing the song "The 3 R's (Respect, Responsibility, Really Good Manners)" by Glenn Colton, noting the letters in the three words.

Notes

_____

_____

_____

_____

_____

_____

_____

_____

_____

_____

Phonics and Structural Analysis

Classroom Activities

A. Given a list of words containing the target sound, children will sound out each word and use it in a sentence.

B. As the teacher says a list of words (with only two thirds containing the target sound), children will sign that letter if they hear the sound or give a "thumbs down" if they do not.

C. Given a word from a current text, students will make as many other words as they can that use only the given letters.

D. On a worksheet or website, children will match contractions with the two words they came from, for example:
don't → do not
she'll → she will

Differentiated Instruction

→ Given a list of picture cards and words containing the target sound, children will sound out each word and match it to its corresponding picture.

→ As the teacher says and writes a list of words (with only two thirds containing the target sound), children will sign the letter for the sound if the sound is present or give "thumbs down" if it is not.

→ Given a *rime* (word family) such as "ing" or "ake," students will make as many other words as they can that follow the rime pattern.

→ On a worksheet or website with a list of similar contractions (e.g., all of them with *'ll* OR *n't*), students will match each contraction to the two words it came from.

Integration of Real-Life Topics

- **Career Awareness/Work Related**
Children will read to reconstruct a sentence (about cooperation and working together) that has been cut apart.

- **Home and Family**
Children will alphabetize a group of items in a food pantry or refrigerator.

- **Leisure Time**
Children will help generate a list of compound words found in sports (e.g., touchdown, basketball).

- **Community Living**
Children will identify rhyming words found in familiar patriotic songs.

- **Emotional/Physical Health**
When reading a big book focusing on friendship (or emotions, health, etc.), the teacher will cover key words for the children to predict and then decode to confirm their prediction.

Notes

_____

_____

_____

_____

_____

_____

_____

_____

_____

Phonics and Structural Analysis

Classroom Activities

A. Given a worksheet or computer program on the "ed" or "ing" ending, the student is to fill in the blank in the sentence with the correct inflection ending (e.g., The dog was drink___ its water).

B. Teams of children will play How Many Words Can You Make? using the same word families (e.g., "ight," "eed," "ake").

C. Presented with a column of words with prefixes (e.g., _rebuild_), students will draw a line to the definition of the word (e.g., "to build again").

D. Children will play Plurals Fishing. Each student will be shown a word (e.g., _kiss_). Student will "fish" (with a fishing pole magnet) for the word with the appropriate plural ending (e.g., _kisses_).

Differentiated Instruction

→ Given a sentence on a sentence strip with a blank, the student is to choose the word with the correct inflection ending to complete the sentence and type it in the blank.

→ The students will be given one word family (e.g., "ake") and must make five new words using that family.

→ Presented with a column of words and column of prefixes, students will draw a line from the prefix to the appropriate root word.

→ The teacher will read a sentence containing a word with a plural ending. Student will come up to the sentence chart and circle the word.

Integration of Real-Life Topics

- **Career Awareness/Work Related**
  Students will alphabetize all of the jobs on the classroom chore chart.

- **Home and Family**
  Given a list of rooms in the home, students will circle the words that are compound words.

- **Leisure Time**
  Students will practice spelling patterns by playing Junior Scrabble, Spellmaster, or Boggle.

- **Community Living**
  Students will finish a partially completed crossword puzzle focused on a community theme (e.g., Memorial Day, Fire Safety) or event.

- **Emotional/Physical Health**
  Given a list of foods on the food pyramid, students will categorize the words into plural nouns and singular nouns.

Notes

_____

_____

_____

_____

_____

_____

_____

_____

Phonics and Structural Analysis

Classroom Activities

A Given a prefix crossword puzzle, students will solve clues to complete each word, including the appropriate prefix.

B. Using a customized computer program containing a variety of suffixes and root words, students will drag and drop the suffix to the correct root word to make a new word.

C. Given a list of word cards (two words to a card), students will write the appropriate contraction underneath the words on the card.

D. Students will be given a word (e.g., *encouragement*). They are to write the prefix, the base word, and the suffix of the word on white boards.

Differentiated Instruction

→ The teacher will read a clue describing a word with a prefix. Students will orally choose the word with a prefix that best matches the clue.

→ Given a variety of root words on chart paper, students will write the appropriate suffix for the root word from a choice of two.

→ The teacher will hold up two words at a time. Students will state the appropriate contraction made from those two words.

→ Given a base word, students will add either a suffix or prefix to the word and will state the new word.

Integration of Real-Life Topics

• **Career Awareness/Work Related**
Students will determine the general category of an unfamiliar career by defining its root word (e.g., *paralegal*).

• **Home and Family**
By analyzing the parts of the words, students will define the meaning of various holiday words (e.g., Thanksgiving; Memorial Day).

• **Emotional/Physical Health**
Students will generate a list of gerunds relating to bullying (e.g., *pushing, teasing, shoving*).

• **Leisure Time**
In the Leisure section of the newspaper, students will find and list multisyllabic words in their own realm of interest.

• **Community Living**
Following a community walk, students will generate a list of compound words from the community (e.g., *crosswalk, skyscraper*).

Notes

_____

_____

_____

_____

_____

_____

_____

_____

_____

_____

Phonics and Structural Analysis

Classroom Activities

A. Students will read flash cards with prefixes, suffixes, and spelling patterns (e.g., "un," "ing," cvvc, cvc). They will discuss various ways the words can be broken apart.

B. Students will play a memory game in which they match a root word with an appropriate superlative ("er," "est").

C. Students will read a selected text and make a list of words that contain the target spelling pattern (e.g., cvvc or cvcc).

D. Students will create a list of compound words made of one common word and another word (e.g., *schoolhouse, household, houseboat*).

Differentiated Instruction

→ Students will read flash cards of words with prefixes, suffixes, and specific spelling patterns that have been highlighted. They will group them by "families."

→ Teams of students will play a memory game in which they match root words with selected superlatives ("er," "est").

→ With a partner, students will read a selection of text and highlight and state words that contain the target spelling pattern.

→ Students will create compound words by combining one common word with others chosen from a list of possibilities.

Integration of Real-Life Topics

• **Career Awareness/Work Related**
Students will explain prefixes and suffixes relating to a chosen career or job (e.g., disengage gears, recheck patient's blood pressure).

• **Home and Family**
Students will generate and discuss synonyms for a home chore chart (e.g., *vacuum* = run the vacuum cleaner; *wipe/wash/clean/dust*).

• **Leisure Time**
Students will follow board- or card-game directions that include familiar contractions (e.g., *you'll, don't*).

• **Community Living**
When grocery shopping, students will read a personalized checklist, noting the variety of plural items. They will purchase accordingly (e.g., 2 lbs. of honey, two heads of lettuce).

• **Emotional/Physical Health**
Students will self-evaluate physical fitness skills using words such as *strong, stronger, strongest, faster, fastest,* and so forth.

Notes

Phonics and Structural Analysis

Classroom Activities

A. Given a list of common suffixes ("ly," "ful," "less"), students will highlight words with those suffixes in a given reading selection.

B. Students will generate sets of homophones and illustrate each word on a separate sheet of paper to make a "Homophones" book to be used with students in a lower grade (e.g., "First-Grade Friends"). As a group they will use their homophones to make the book into a class story.

C. Given a current text selection, students will find, list, and categorize words under the appropriate heading (e.g., "Root Words," "Compound Words," "Acronyms/Initials").

D. Given a list of multisyllabic words, students will break apart each word to show its syllables and will generate lists of two-, three-, and four-syllable words.

Differentiated Instruction

→ In small groups, students will create a wall chart depicting root words _with_ suffixes and those words separated from their suffixes (e.g., _quietly_ = "quiet" + "ly").

→ Working in pairs, students will be given a set of homophones and will illustrate their words and then insert those words in the appropriate spot in a teacher-made story.

→ After reading a current text, students will be given a set of word cards from the text to categorize under the appropriate heading (e.g., "Root Words," "Compound Words," "Acronyms/Initials").

→ Given a list of multisyllabic words already broken into their syllables, students will re-form the words, say them, and place them on a class chart to show lists of two-, three-, and four-syllable words.

Integration of Real-Life Topics

- **Career Awareness/Work Related**
  Given a list of career words (e.g., _psychologist, photographer, cashier_), students will analyze each word to determine its root as a clue to determining the nature of the career.

- **Home and Family**
  Students will "inventory" tools, utensils, and appliances at home to later add to a class chart of compound words, multisyllabic words, singular words, plurals, and so forth.

- **Leisure Time**
  Students will use as many synonyms as possible to write a paragraph describing a favorite indoor or outdoor activity. They will illustrate their paragraph for a class book.

- **Community Living**
  While visiting a community activity or location (e.g., mall, athletic event, video store), students will generate a list of words with diphthongs or digraphs to later add to a class list for study.

- **Emotional/Physical Health**
  Students will generate a list of emotion words with superlatives (e.g., _sad, sadder, saddest_). They will create and act out a skit based on one of the words, and their peers will guess which word is featured.

Notes

_____

_____

_____

_____

_____

_____

_____

_____

_____

_____

_____

_____

Sight Word and Vocabulary Development

Classroom Activities

A. Pairs of children will toss a beanbag onto large word cards on the floor. If a child can read the word, he or she gets a point. If not, the other player will have a chance to read the same word.

B. Children will group cards with sight words according to beginning sound, final sound, or vowel (or relevant topical category).

C. Children will write a book titled *I See, We See, I Like, I Can*. Each child inserts an appropriate noun or verb and illustrates each page.

D. Children will play the game Red Rover, with each child wearing a sight word on a large paper sign. The other team says "Red Rover, Red Rover, send [sight word] over!" The child wearing that word tries to run to the other team.

Differentiated Instruction

→ As a team, students will toss a beanbag onto large word cards on the floor. The team will read the word and use it in a sentence.

→ Children will place sight words into the correct labeled basket (e.g., "s words," "words with e").

→ As a class, the children will author a book titled *I See . . .* (or, e.g., *We See . . . , I Like . . .*) Each child will compose a page, and the book will be read together as a class.

→ With assistance from a peer partner, children will play Red Rover while wearing a sight word on a large paper sign. The other team says "Red Rover, Red Rover, send [sight word] over!" Child wearing that word tries to run to the other team.

Integration of Real-Life Topics

- **Career Awareness/Work Related**
  Students will explain with words and/or actions the role of a given school employee when shown a photo of that person.

- **Home and Family**
  While setting a table, children will identify the name of each item in a place setting.

- **Leisure Time**
  While viewing a PowerPoint presentation showing various sports and activities, children will name and briefly explain an activity.

- **Community Living**
  During a neighborhood walk, children will identify various community helpers as they pass the appropriate building.

- **Emotional/Physical Health**
  Using a teacher-made big book depicting various social scenarios, children will state the probable feelings associated with scenario (e.g., birthday party → *excited*).

Notes

_____

_____

_____

_____

_____

_____

_____

_____

_____

_____

READING / Word Study

Sight Word and Vocabulary Development

Classroom Activities

A. Using a website (e.g., www.manatee.k12.fl.us), students will match pictures with the appropriate sight word on a Bingo-like matching game.

B. Children will read sight words on the sides of a large sight-word die when rolled. The teacher can hide the die and have children say, spell, and use the word in a sentence.

C. Children will be given a paper plate with a small mound of pudding on it. The teacher will call out sight words, and students will use fingers to write the word in the pudding.

D. With a partner, children will play Go Fish with sight word cards to "acquire" pairs of sight words.

Differentiated Instruction

→ Given a set of picture cards, students will match sight words with the appropriate picture.

→ Teacher will roll a large die that has pictures on each side. Children will state the sight word that corresponds with the picture. They will point to the word on a word wall.

→ Children will be given a paper plate with a small mound of pudding on it. As the teacher calls out each sight word, children will chorally spell the word and individually use fingers to spell the word in pudding.

→ Children will play Sight Word Concentration, in which they match pairs of sight words.

Integration of Real-Life Topics

- **Career Awareness/Work Related**
  Each student will identify his or her own classroom job by using labeled photographs and placing his or her own name card with the job.

- **Home and Family**
  Students will match word cards (with or without picture clues) with a room in the home or an object in the home (e.g., *table, closet*).

- **Leisure Time**
  Students will categorize a group of games/sports/ hobbies by placing a labeled picture under one of two headings: "Indoor" or "Outdoor."

- **Community Living**
  Students will act out an emergency situation and identify the appropriate community service to contact by holding up a word card with that service's "name" (e.g., *police, plumber, ambulance*).

- **Emotional/Physical Health**
  Students will identify various items as "safe" or "not safe." They will place pictures or photos (with or without words) under a ☺ category or a ☹ category.

Notes

_____

_____

_____

_____

_____

_____

_____

_____

_____

_____

_____

_____

Sight Word and Vocabulary Development

Classroom Activities

A. Each student will be provided with a Sight Word Bingo card. The teacher will select an index card with a sight word on it. Students will place a chip on the sight word if it appears on their card until someone gets Bingo.

B. Given white boards, markers, and up to five clues that describe a particular vocabulary word, each student will race to write the word on his or her white board.

C. Using magnetic letters, students will unscramble letters in a sight word and state the sight word when asked.

D. Students will locate and circle sight words found in a current content area text. They can then compare their found words with those of a partner.

Differentiated Instruction

→ The class will be divided into two teams. Teacher will hold up a sight word. One member of the team states the word. Each team receives one point for each correct word.

→ The teacher will hand a student an index card with a sight word on it. The student will locate the word on the word wall, point to it, and say the word.

→ Using magnetic letters, students will fill in the missing letter of a sight word, then state the sight word.

→ Students will locate a stated sight word placed in the room on a large index card. When located, the student must restate the word and place it on the word wall.

Integration of Real-Life Topics

• **Career Awareness/Work Related**
The class will visit a community-based worksite (e.g., grocery store). Students will locate common sight words at the worksite (e.g., *exit, keep out, men*).

• **Home and Family**
Given home jobs/chores listed on a job chart, students will read their assigned job and explain the responsibilities and tasks associated with the job.

• **Leisure Time**
The class will dictate (together) a story about a favorite leisure-time activity. The story must include sight words recently learned, and during a rereading, students will indicate the word(s) used.

• **Community Living**
Students will take a walking tour of their community. When coming upon a common sign with a sight word, students will check off that sight word on a checklist.

• **Emotional/Physical Health**
Presented with sight words that represent emotions (e.g., *happy, sad*), students will state the sight word, act out the emotion, and tell of a time or situation when that emotion was felt.

Notes

Sight Word and Vocabulary Development

Classroom Activities

A. Students will write a sight word and its definition, stated by the teacher, in their writing journals. They will then illustrate each word or use it in a sentence.

B. Given a paragraph with missing words (sight words or vocabulary), students will complete the sentence with the sight word that best fits the paragraph's meaning.

C. Students will read a paragraph on a current topic of study or interest and will list and tally the sight words found in the paragraph.

D. Students will be given a worksheet with a picture of a sight/vocabulary word and several possible spellings of it. The students will circle the correct spelling of the word that represents the picture.

Differentiated Instruction

→ Students will trace each sight word on a worksheet. When worksheets are completed, the teacher will have the students state the sight word and its meaning.

→ As a group, students will circle learned sight or vocabulary words in a paragraph presented on a chart. The teacher will then hold up the word on an index card, and students will provide a definition for the word.

→ Students will read sentences with a word missing on a worksheet and circle the appropriate sight/vocabulary word to fill in the blank.

→ Students will be given a worksheet with sight words and pictures. Students will draw a line from the word to the correct picture.

Integration of Real-Life Topics

• **Career Awareness/Work Related**
Students will be shown pictures of various occupational tools. They will name the career in which the tools are used.

• **Home and Family**
The teacher will hold up a generic picture of a family member. The students must state the sight/vocabulary word that best represents the picture (e.g., *brother*).

• **Leisure Time**
The teacher will read a description of a number of activities related to a sport. Students will hold up the vocabulary word card best related to the sport's description (e.g., "He scored a goal with the *puck*" [hockey]).

• **Community Living**
Students will read together a *Weekly Reader* article about community responsibilities (e.g., not littering). At the end of the reading, students will identify key vocabulary words in the reading and state their meanings.

• **Emotional/Physical Health**
Students will match anatomy vocabulary to the body system of which it is a part to create a chart of all of the body's systems.

Notes

Sight Word and Vocabulary Development

Classroom Activities

A. Students will view a teacher-made audiovisual (AV) presentation that previews key sight words from a text. Pairs of students will then play a series of games to practice those words.

B. Using premade vocabulary word cards, students will match each card with a paragraph from a page in which the word was used.

C. Students will locate key sight words in a given text (chart, paragraph, chapter) and present the location of the word to their class.

D. Given a class-made time line depicting a sequence of events, students will match vocabulary word cards with specific events.

Differentiated Instruction

→ After viewing a teacher-made AV presentation that previews key sight words, students will play a series of games in a guided group to practice those words.

→ Using premade vocabulary word cards, students will match each card with a picture depicting a story event in which the word was used.

→ Student pairs will be given sight word cards. Each student will illustrate his or her word, and then the partner will match the illustration with the corresponding sight word.

→ Given a class-made time line depicting a sequence of familiar events, students will unscramble vocabulary word cards to correspond with the time line and events.

Integration of Real-Life Topics

• **Career Awareness/Work Related**
Students will compare and contrast specific words depicting various occupations identified in a given text (any time frame or subject area).

• **Home and Family**
Students will prepare a Venn diagram using current vocabulary words to depict the similarities and differences between families of various cultures.

• **Leisure Time**
On an appropriate map, students will locate the names of places they would like to visit.

• **Community Living**
Students will match or illustrate a picture of community signs and symbols. They will match the appropriate word with the illustration or symbol.

• **Emotional/Physical Health**
From a list, students will choose the vocabulary word that best corresponds to a given scenario depicting an aspect of physical and/or emotional health.

Notes

_____

_____

_____

_____

_____

_____

_____

_____

_____

_____

GRADE 5

Sight Word and Vocabulary Development

Classroom Activities

A. Given a list of key words in a text, students will categorize each word according to its word type (e.g., noun, verb, adjective, adverb) and add each word to a class word-type chart.

B. Given a list of unfamiliar multisyllabic words, students will locate each word in their text. They will then discuss meanings as per the text.

C. Students will create a series of word webs structured by headings, topics, and subtopics. They will then illustrate each word or group of words.

D. To provide practice for their peers, students will develop and make a game board to practice vocabulary words from a current text.

Differentiated Instruction

→ Given cards of illustrated key words from a text, small groups of students will categorize each word according to its word type (e.g., noun, verb, adjective) and place each card in the correct category on a class chart.

→ Given a list of unfamiliar words, students will find each word in the text. They will categorize each word by topic, subtopic, paragraph, and so forth.

→ Given a series of word webs structured according to a current text topic, students will find one word on each web that does not fit.

→ To provide practice for their peers, small groups will create a chart, bulletin board, or poster highlighting a vocabulary word (or words) from a current text.

Integration of Real-Life Topics

- **Career Awareness/Work Related**
  Students will create a list of words pertaining to a specific career. They will use those words to search on the Internet for more information about the career.

- **Home and Family**
  Students will create a home emergency kit (for first aid, power outage, or a natural disaster). They will list each item in the kit and describe its use.

- **Leisure Time**
  Using the Internet, newspapers, and/or magazines, students will locate travel advertisements. They will categorize the words on the ads according to the current topic of study (e.g., continents, cities, historic sites).

- **Community Living**
  Given information about various public emergency services available in the community, students will use key words to categorize the information according to type of service (e.g., public safety, health). Students will compile the data in an information packet for community members.

- **Emotional/Physical Health**
  As part of a health unit or a parenting class, students will identify key symptoms for recognizing a disease or illness. They can list the key symptoms according to illness and again according to treatment options.

Notes

_____

_____

_____

_____

_____

_____

_____

_____

_____

_____

_____

_____

_____

_____

_____

Context Clues and Reference Sources

Classroom Activities

A. As a prereading exercise, children will be taught to visualize story events as they read. The teacher will read a series of descriptive phrases for the children to mentally picture. Each child will discuss what he or she "saw."

B. The teacher will create a riddle book showing photos or artifacts and emblems from various local businesses (drugstore, restaurant, grocery store). On one side of the page, the artifacts are shown, and on the other side is a photo or picture of the business' sign. Children will "read" the clues to identify the business.

C. The teacher will read a series of sentences about the current topic/story. Each sentence will be missing one (content-related) word. Children will choose a picture to represent the missing word.

D. A small group of children will act out a brief scenario that clearly evokes a specific emotion. The rest of the class will give the skit a title that includes the name of the emotion.

Differentiated Instruction

→ As a prereading exercise, children will be taught to visualize story events as they read. The teacher will read a descriptive phrase and direct the children to visualize certain aspects of the phrase (e.g., "The snow was glistening"). The teacher says, "Picture snow, big piles of white snow. Glistening snow sparkles—picture sparkling snow."

→ Students will match photos of artifacts and emblems from various local businesses to a picture of the business. They will cut and paste the pictures to help create a riddle book for their peers.

→ The teacher will read one sentence with a word missing. Students will choose which of three pictures best represents the missing word.

→ Children will be shown several pictures that clearly evoke a specific emotion. Children will discuss and name the emotion.

Integration of Real-Life Topics

• **Career Awareness/Work Related**
The teacher will read a description of a particular career scenario. Students will hold up a puppet corresponding to that career.

• **Home and Family**
At home, children will find x number of items fitting a particular category (e.g., items with motors, soft items, pet supplies) and state the room where each was found.

• **Leisure Time**
Children will create a drawing to show the equipment/gear needed for a particular sport, game, or activity.

• **Community Living**
Students will be shown examples of environmental print (e.g., stop sign, restaurant name logo). Students will identify the sign and discuss how they know what it says.

• **Emotional/Physical Health**
When shown photos of children's behavior during daily situations (e.g., eating breakfast, riding the school

bus, playing with a friend), children will show a happy face card or a sad face card to show if the behavior(s) shown is/are appropriate.

Notes

_____

_____

_____

_____

_____

_____

_____

_____

_____

_____

Context Clues and Reference Sources

Classroom Activities

A. Using a website such as factmonster.com or kidskonnect.com, students will find three facts about a chosen animal. The facts will be written in a brief "Animal Report."

B. Students will be "Word Detectives," using pictures and sense of the story to determine an unknown word in a sentence (e.g., "The boy put on his pajamas and hopped into _____"). They will discuss their reasoning.

C. The teacher will display a chart of a short story describing but not directly identifying a school activity. Children will highlight and discuss words that gave them clues to identify the activity.

D. Upon encountering an unfamiliar and unknown word, students will say "blank" for the word and read to the end of the sentence. The teacher and the students will discuss contextual clues (semantic and syntactic) to decipher the word.

Differentiated Instruction

→ Using a teacher-made chart describing a given animal, students will choose three facts about the animal to be included in a class "Animal Report."

→ Students will complete a teacher-directed picture walk through a new text. The teacher will direct students' attention to any new or unfamiliar words.

→ The teacher will display and read a series of short riddles, with each riddle describing a classroom activity. Students will discuss each and identify the activity.

→ Upon encountering an unfamiliar word, students will be shown three pictures, one picture of which identifies the word. They will choose a picture, using and discussing possible clues, to identify the word.

Integration of Real-Life Topics

• **Career Awareness/Work Related**
While showing a large photo or poster depicting a familiar job/career, the teacher will read four word cards (three related to the career and one unrelated). Children will choose the one that does not belong and explain their reasoning.

• **Home and Family**
Students will read a one- or two-sentence scenario of a home activity (e.g., eating breakfast, taking a bath, walking the dog). They will identify the part of the day—morning, afternoon, evening—in which the activity occurs.

• **Leisure Time**
Children will make a list of clothing or supplies needed to play outdoors during a particular season (e.g., hat, mittens, boots, etc., in winter).

• **Community Living**
Children will read a brief story about a community event (where a danger or safety issue occurs). They will then discuss the words that led them to "see" the danger.

• **Emotional/Physical Health**
While reading a "food-related story" (such as *Bread and Jam for Frances*) children will stop and make suggestions as to healthy/healthier food choices.

Notes

_____
_____
_____
_____
_____
_____
_____
_____
_____
_____
_____
_____
_____

Context Clues and Reference Sources

Classroom Activities

A. The teacher will display words with multiple meanings (e.g., *bat*). He or she will explain that it is often difficult to determine the exact meaning of a word until it is used in context. Students will be presented with a sentence that includes an underlined word that has multiple meanings. Students will read the sentence and explain which meaning applies.

B. Students will read a sentence with an underlined multiple-meaning word. When presented with three or four other sentences with that word, they will select the sentence in which the word has the same meaning as in the original sentence.

C. Students will complete a chart showing information they would like to learn about a given topic. They will use a children's search engine (e.g., yahooligans.com, kidsclick.org, netnanny.com) to find the desired information.

D. Students will read a silly poem that highlights a given topic. Classmates will use context clues and hints from the poem to determine the topic presented.

Differentiated Instruction

→ Out of a hat, students will pull a word with multiple meanings. Students will place the word in each of two or three sentences to test its meaning and determine which sentence best shows one meaning of the word.

→ Students will be given a sentence containing an underlined multiple-meaning word. They will match the sentence with a picture depicting the appropriate meaning for the given context of the word.

→ Pairs of students will locate specific facts on a given topic using a predetermined website (e.g., factmonster.com, kids.yahoo.com).

→ Students will listen to a silly poem that highlights a given topic. Students will select a word card and/or illustration that depicts the given topic.

Integration of Real-Life Topics

• **Career Awareness/Work Related**
Students will be assigned various classroom jobs on a job chart. Students will use picture clues to help them remember the components of the job they are to perform.

• **Home and Family**
Students will read the sequence of tasks involved in laundering clothes. They will use included contextual clues and pictures to determine each step of the process.

• **Leisure Time**
In preparation for a field trip to a local restaurant, students will be provided with a menu. They will write down any unfamiliar words and use context clues in the menu (e.g., headings, photos) to help determine the words' meanings.

• **Community Living**
As a homework project, students (with adult assistance) will compile a list of key community emergency services and each service's contact information.

• **Emotional/Physical Health**
Students will be presented with various pictures of appropriate/inappropriate ways of maintaining their personal health/appearance. The students will explain which are appropriate and which are inappropriate.

Notes

_____

_____

_____

_____

_____

_____

_____

_____

GRADE 3

Context Clues and Reference Sources

Classroom Activities

A. After reading a paragraph, the students will answer questions regarding the reading (e.g., "What does the word *identify* mean?"). The students will underline the context clue in the paragraph that gives them the meaning of the word (e.g., "means to . . .").

B. Students will trade and read their own *cloze* stories. Students will fill in the blanks of the story from a given word list.

C. Students will be given a list of new vocabulary words. They will use the dictionary to locate the meanings of the words and write and illustrate the definitions, which will be put on a classroom bulletin board.

D. Students will develop a series of questions to ask an armed forces veteran. They will then interview the person and write down the responses to the questions.

Differentiated Instruction

→ The teacher will read aloud a sentence strip, pointing out the underlined word. The teacher will have the students read the same sentence, tell what the underlined word means, and state how they determined the meaning.

→ Given a worksheet with sentences on it, with each sentence containing one blank, students will circle the appropriate word for the blank from a choice of three words.

→ Students will be given new vocabulary words and use a child's online dictionary to locate the meaning of the words. The students will cut and paste illustrations onto a word-processing document to share with their classmates.

→ The teacher will provide pairs of students with two to three interview questions. The students will pose the questions to a veteran and record the responses.

Integration of Real-Life Topics

• **Career Awareness/Work Related**
Students will read job descriptions for various occupations. They will use the dictionary to define any unfamiliar words. They will then give brief oral reports to describe and explain the careers.

• **Home and Family**
Students will use a recipe book to plan and make a simple, balanced lunch.

• **Leisure Time**
Students will use the newspaper to read about an event coming to town (e.g., musical group performance). The students will use the Internet to find out more about the group and its members.

• **Community Living**
Students will discuss the importance of upcoming elections. They will use various reference materials (e.g., Internet sites, interviews) to learn about the candidates and create a campaign poster for one of the candidates.

• **Emotional/Physical Health**
Students will read a short paragraph on a health topic in which the key words (e.g., *emotional, adversity*) are underlined. Students will use context clues to

determine the meaning of each word and write the definitions in their health journals.

Notes

_____

_____

_____

_____

_____

_____

_____

_____

_____

_____

Context Clues and Reference Sources

Classroom Activities

A. While reading a specific text, students will circle any unknown words and underline words or phrases that they think will assist in defining the word. The teacher will lead a discussion about the words and their context clues.

B. Given a chart of similes and metaphors, students will create new comparisons (i.e., new similes/ metaphors) to show that they understand the original phrase.

C. Given a teacher-made paragraph with nonsense words substituted for key words, students will determine the "real" key word and explain the clues provided by the text.

D. Given a set of questions on a particular topic, students will use reference sources, such as a dictionary, thesaurus, textbook, or website, to answer the questions and help complete a class-made study guide.

Differentiated Instruction

→ The teacher will read a passage to the students in a guided reading group. When an unknown word is encountered, student will raise his or her hand. The teacher and students will locate words or phrases that assist in defining the word.

→ In art class, students will be given a metaphor to use in creating a collage, painting, poster, and so forth, to depict the meaning of the metaphor.

→ Given the description of a classroom task that contains a difficult word, students will formulate a synonymous description using more familiar words. Classmates will guess the task and the "difficult" word as the task is acted out.

→ Given a set of specific questions on a specific topic, small groups of students will list key words pertaining to each question. They will also determine the best reference source to use.

Integration of Real-Life Topics

• **Career Awareness/Work Related**
After reading selections about a new career, students will generate a list of key words/descriptors for further research, culminating in a PowerPoint presentation to the class.

• **Home and Family**
Students will read a selection about a family vacation, journey, or cross-country trip. Using information from the selection, they will create a set of fictitious postcards that chronicle the geography, landmarks, and specific information on various "stops" along the journey.

• **Leisure Time**
Students will read an article in a sports magazine for children or in a newspaper sports section. From the article, they will compile a list of vivid words and descriptions to create riddles for their classmates to solve (e.g., "What sport is this?" "What athlete is this?")

• **Community Living**
Students will research local community history and create a town time line depicting events, dates, and relevant names.

• **Emotional/Physical Health**
Students will find graphic examples (i.e., pictures/

photographs) that depict the health effects of a natural disaster, such as a wildfire or hurricane.

Notes

_____

_____

_____

_____

_____

_____

_____

_____

_____

_____

_____

READING / Word Study

Context Clues and Reference Sources

Classroom Activities

A. The teacher will show the class a chart showing six categories of context clues (definitions, antonyms, synonyms, use in a series, general context, appositives). Students will locate their vocabulary words in the text and explain which context clue category led them to the word's meaning.

B. Students will be given pairs of homophones. They will determine which word "fits" the text and pantomime for classmates to identify the word and its meaning.

C. Given a set of words with multiple meanings, analogies, or word families, students will define each word by using context clues and then confirm their definition with a dictionary.

D. Given a list of reference sources within their textbook (e.g., table of contents, index, glossary, charts, diagrams, pictures) students will identify a "piece" of information that came from each source. They will explain how they used each source.

Differentiated Instruction

→ Small groups of students will be given a list of words fitting one context clue category and the chart of context clue "categories." They will locate each word and state which category led them to the word's meaning.

→ Pairs of students will be given one pair of homophones. They will determine which word "fits" the text and illustrate that word to show its meaning.

→ In a series of learning centers, students will work in groups to practice applying the use of context clues. They will (a) locate a word in the text to find its meaning, (b) draw a representation of an analogy and match it to the correct word, and (c) use a thesaurus to locate and write a list of synonyms.

→ Given a list of reference sources within their textbook and a set of questions, students will locate the answer to each question and tell which source was used and how it was used.

Integration of Real-Life Topics

• **Career Awareness/Work Related**
Using guide words in an online encyclopedia, students will locate a career of interest and then describe that career in a brief report.

• **Home and Family**
After interviewing a family member about an historic event, students will use terms from the oral history to guide further research on the topic.

• **Leisure Time**
Using travel posters or brochures, students will locate key words about a travel destination. They will use those words to create a riddle. Their peers will guess the travel destination from clues in the riddle.

• **Community Living**
Provided with a list of community services, students will use various community resources (e.g., telephone directory, newspaper, shopping ads) to locate information about each service.

• **Emotional/Physical Health**
Using the contents guide in a newspaper or periodical, students will locate key words focused on a specific

health topic. They will use those key words as guides to focus further research on that topic.

Notes

_____

_____

_____

_____

_____

_____

_____

_____

_____

_____

Predicting/Drawing Conclusions/Making Inferences

Classroom Activities

A. Given a choice of three pictures, students will discuss them and decide which picture shows the probable end of a story being read by the teacher.

B. The teacher and class will read the title and discuss the cover art of a picture book. They will predict the topic of the book, writing predictions on chart paper. They will tally predictions to determine the one most children predicted. Following the story, they will discuss which predictions were closest to the actual storyline.

C. After reading several Laura Numeroff *If You Give a . . .* stories, students will make a class book titled, "If You Give a Kindergartener a . . ."

D. After listening to one or two stories on the topic of an upcoming field trip, students will predict what they will see, experience, do, and so forth, on the trip by writing a sentence.

Differentiated Instruction

→ Given a choice of three unrelated pictures, students will choose the one that depicts the story being read.

→ Through movement or facial expressions, students will depict the predicted emotions of a main character after reading the title and discussing the cover art.

→ Each student will illustrate a page in a class book with the title, "If You Give a Kindergartener a . . ."

→ After discussing an upcoming field trip, students will draw a picture of one thing they think they will see, and the teacher will write a dictated caption for it.

Integration of Real-Life Topics

• **Career Awareness/Work Related**
Students will identify careers by the uniform or gear the workers wear.

• **Home and Family**
Children will predict the day on which the next load of laundry must be done based on the current "status" of the hamper.

• **Leisure Time**
Children will predict and plan a menu for a class picnic. They will predict how hungry the class will be and decide on what to pack.

• **Community Living**
After watching a movie about Earth Day and walking through the community, students will decide whether a community clean-up day is needed.

• **Emotional/Physical Health**
Children will predict the likely outcome of not brushing one's teeth.

Notes

_____

_____

_____

_____

_____

_____

_____

_____

READING / Comprehension

Predicting/Drawing Conclusions/Making Inferences

Classroom Activities

A. The teacher and students will discuss an action-filled picture and choose (from a list of four sentences) the sentence that tells what will probably happen next. They will discuss their rationale.

B. As a class, students write predictions for the ending of a story currently being read. Reading will continue, and the class will note any emerging "clues" that refute or support their predictions.

C. Students will read and discuss several "if . . . then . . ." statements and fill in missing "then" words and phrases on a teacher-made chart.

D. Students will complete a chart titled "Predictions and Evidence." While reading, they will stop two to three times to predict again and add their ideas to the chart.

Differentiated Instruction

→ After discussing an action-filled picture, students will choose (from a set of two to four pictures) the picture that shows what will happen next.

→ While reading and discussing a story, students and teacher will generate a prediction and find two or three story clues to support the prediction.

→ Students will listen to and discuss several "if . . . then . . ." statements and choose a word card to fill in the missing "then" words on a teacher-made chart.

→ The teacher and students will complete a chart titled "Predictions and Evidence." The teacher will stop two to three times during reading to refer to the chart and have the children predict again, discussing their ideas.

Integration of Real-Life Topics

• **Career Awareness/Work Related**
Students will determine a career being discussed by solving a set of riddles that describe functions, jobs, uniform, and so forth, of the career.

• **Home and Family**
Students will determine what to wear to school based on a parent's description of the weather and the day's planned activities.

• **Leisure Time**
Children will predict which booth at the community fair will be most crowded based on the teacher and classmates' discussion of their own plans for visiting the fair.

• **Community Living**
After the teacher's identification and presentation of a classroom problem, students will generate a new classroom rule.

• **Emotional/Physical Health**
Children will determine the relative safety of new playground equipment and will generate safety rules for the equipment.

Notes

_____

_____

_____

_____

_____

_____

_____

_____

_____

_____

_____

Predicting/Drawing Conclusions/Making Inferences

Classroom Activities

A. Given 10 preselected words from a story and worksheet titled "Can You Predict the Story?" students will predict in which section each word may fit (e.g., setting, problem).

B. After reading a story with a surprise ending, students will illustrate the beginning and write a prediction question for classmates to "guess" the answer (e.g., "Where will the princess go?").

C. After reading one or two versions of a familiar story (e.g., variations of *The Three Little Pigs*) and discussing the plot, especially the ending, students will read another version and predict the ending.

D. After reading a story with an unexpected ending, students will discuss possible plot changes and predict alternate endings ("What would happen if . . .").

Differentiated Instruction

→ Given a set of pictures from a story, students will make a group poster, placing various story illustrations in a "story element" section of the poster (e.g., setting, characters) and predicting and discussing where each picture may fit.

→ After reading a story with a surprise ending, students will illustrate the answer to a prediction question such as, "Where will the prince find the dragon?"

→ After having read several familiar stories about the same topic (e.g., school, cats, baseball), students will read another similar story and predict the ending.

→ Students and teacher will discuss an alternative ending to a familiar story by asking, "What would happen if . . . ." They will then act out the new ending.

Integration of Real-Life Topics

• **Career Awareness/Work Related**
After learning about a career, students will determine appropriate work habits and behavior for that career.

• **Home and Family**
When arranging furniture, students will predict outcomes of various furniture arrangements (e.g., traffic flow, convenience, safety).

• **Leisure Time**
Students will listen to a familiar song, predict a possible next verse, and write the new verse. Later, they can perform the reworked song as a skit.

• **Community Living**
Students will plan an appropriate celebration for an upcoming school or community event or holiday and create a list of needed supplies.

• **Emotional/Physical Health**
Students will discuss the signs and signals that indicate a classmate is not feeling well.

Notes

_____

_____

_____

_____

_____

_____

_____

_____

_____

Predicting/Drawing Conclusions/Making Inferences

READING / Comprehension

Classroom Activities

A. Students will read the first two pages of a chapter. The teacher will ask, "What would you expect the rest of the chapter to be about?" Students will provide sensible evidence for their predictions.

B. Students will be shown pictures of significant local or national monuments or memorials. They will make inferences as to their meaning and significance. They will write their thoughts and compare them with those of a partner.

C. Students will read different versions of the same folk tale. They will draw a conclusion indicating the central theme and make a collage to illustrate that theme.

D. Students will read a biography of a famous person, determine the underlying theme or central message of his or her life/work, and give examples of actions their person might do, given his or her theme or message.

Differentiated Instruction

→ Students will examine pictures (from a book with only a few) and make predictions as to the topic of the book.

→ Students will read a (children's) news article about monuments and memorials and will discuss their thoughts about the reason(s) the monument exists.

→ The teacher will read aloud a folk tale and will discuss it with students. Students will draw a conclusion as to the theme of the folk tale. They will identify pictures from the story that clearly exemplify the theme.

→ Students will listen to a biography and answer inferential questions posed by the teacher (e.g., "What does the author/character mean when . . . ?"). They will work together (in groups or pairs) to decide on the central message and/or main component of the person's work.

Integration of Real-Life Topics

• **Career Awareness/Work Related**
Children will examine pictures of people doing various jobs and predict what would come next in the process/job depicted.

• **Home and Family**
When shown unsafe home situations with captions, students will read the caption, decide why the situation is unsafe, and suggest how it could be remedied to be safe.

• **Leisure Time**
A family member will read aloud the directions to a common game. The student will determine the object of the game.

• **Community Living**
Students will take a walk through their community, paying particular attention to safety signs. Students will decide why the signs, in general, are important.

• **Emotional/Physical Health**
Children will watch an exercise DVD and determine why this particular exercise is beneficial.

Notes

_____

_____

_____

_____

_____

_____

_____

_____

_____

_____

_____

Predicting/Drawing Conclusions/Making Inferences

Classroom Activities

A. Students will examine (in a text) the physical characteristics and behaviors of a given animal and will draw a conclusion as to the animal's habitat so they can draw a picture of that habitat.

B. Students will use newspaper headlines to make inferences about newspaper stories' topics and main points. They will create a memory game that matches headlines with topics.

C. Students will select two to four familiar and unfamiliar proverbs, sayings, or phrases from a list. They will infer unknown meanings to explain the saying to the class (e.g., "A watched pot never boils").

D. After participating in a directed reading of a fictional story about weather, students will predict future weather events for the story and write a continuation of it.

Differentiated Instruction

→ After examining (in a text) the physical characteristics and behaviors of a given animal, students will match a labeled picture of the animal to a labeled picture of its habitat.

→ Students will use newspaper photographs with headlines to infer the articles' topics and main points. They will create illustrations to mimic each photograph.

→ In pairs, students will draw or act out the inferred meaning of an unfamiliar saying, phrase, or proverb.

→ The teacher will read a fictional story about weather. Given a set of three real-life photos of weather (e.g., from newspapers, the Internet), students will choose the photo that accurately predicts the ending of the story.

Integration of Real-Life Topics

- **Career Awareness/Work Related**
  Students will generate a chart of careers that require a given amount of education or training.

- **Home and Family**
  Students will predict the potential usefulness of a laptop computer with the goal of convincing a parent to purchase one.

- **Leisure Time**
  Students will determine the number of games or activities needed to occupy themselves on a 3-hour car ride.

- **Community Living**
  After having read a sample menu, students will determine the type of restaurant from which the menu came (e.g., fast food, Mexican, diner).

- **Emotional/Physical Health**
  In a mock emergency, students will determine the proper course of action that should be taken by each individual.

Notes

_____

_____

_____

_____

_____

_____

_____

_____

_____

_____

GRADE 5

READING / Comprehension

Predicting/Drawing Conclusions/Making Inferences

Classroom Activities

A. Given a story title, initial paragraph, and cover art, students will write a list of questions that are likely to be answered in text.

B. Provided with a list of new vocabulary words and phrases used in a story, students will find specific context details (other words, phrases, captions) to define each word or phrase. They will choose one word and make a small sign to show and describe the definition of the word.

C. Students will use beginning story events and previous personal experiences to make specific predictions about the main character's feelings and actions. They will create a chart to compare their initial predictions with actual story outcomes.

D. At the end of a unit of study on a novel, students will develop a story web that answers the following questions:
   1. What story details or events surprised you?
   2. How did your initial view of the main character(s) change?
   3. At what point(s) in the story did your prediction change?

Differentiated Instruction

→ After previewing a story, students will generate "who," "what," "where," and "when" questions (on "cue cards") for the story. These can later be used to quiz one another on actual story events.

→ Students will use a "synonym card" to define each new vocabulary word. If further prompts are needed, a picture clue will be put on the reverse side of each card.

→ With a partner, students will develop a picture sequence to show the main character's actions from the beginning to the end of the story.

→ Provided with a teacher-made web/outline and specific details on sentence strips, students will match story details to the story elements and their reactions on the outline.

Integration of Real-Life Topics

• **Career Awareness/Work Related**
Students will make inferences as to the various responsibilities of a given worker and then confirm or refute their inferences based on research on the given career area (e.g., farming, astronomy, biology, technology, meteorology).

• **Home and Family**
Given a family history relative to immigration and geography, students will make an inference to explain a family's geographical movement.

• **Leisure Time**
After a family responds to a "Vacation Options Survey," students will decide on the location of the best vacation destination and recreational activities to pursue.

• **Community Living**
Provided with a description of services offered by various community agencies and businesses, students will match the descriptions with business cards that identify the type and name of the service.

• **Emotional/Physical Health**
Each student will contribute to a class "emergency manual." This manual will be used to prevent, prepare for, and survive a variety of potential emergencies.

Notes

_____

_____

_____

_____

_____

_____

_____

_____

Main Idea

Classroom Activities

A. After listening to a story, children will draw a picture for the book cover.

B. After listening to a read-aloud story, students will orally state a title for the story.

C. Students will together generate a main idea sentence for a set of related pictures.

D. Following a read-aloud story, students will identify a sentence that does not belong in the story.

Differentiated Instruction

→ After listening to a story, children will choose, from a set of three pictures, a picture that would make a good cover and color it.

→ After listening to a read-aloud story, children will choose the best title for a story from a list of three titles.

→ Students will circle words on the chalkboard that tell about a set of related pictures.

→ Following a read-aloud story, children will cross out the picture (out of four pictures) that does not tell about the story.

Integration of Real-Life Topics

• **Career Awareness/Work Related**
Children will cut out magazine photographs to add to a class collage of careers.

• **Home and Family**
After a family game night, children will bring in the game and explain the purpose of it during Show and Tell.

• **Leisure Time**
After singing a familiar song, children will draw a picture to represent the topic of the song. They will explain their picture to the class.

• **Community Living**
Children will draw a picture of a bus safety rule. With assistance, they will write the name of the rule on their picture.

• **Emotional/Physical Health**
Children will choose the healthy snacks from a poster of mixed snacks. They will discuss the differences between the healthy and unhealthy snacks.

Notes

_____

_____

_____

_____

_____

_____

_____

_____

_____

_____

Main Idea

Classroom Activities

A. Children will read four sentences and decide which three would go together. Each child will write and illustrate a main idea statement

B. Children will read a list of 10 words and group them into two categories. They will discuss possible main idea statements for each group of words.

C. After listening to a story, students will discuss the "who," "what," "where," and "when" aspects of the story to create a group story map.

D. After reading a short story, children will circle 3 words, from a list of 10 to 12, that best explain the main idea.

Differentiated Instruction

→ As a group, children will read four sentences and discuss and decide which three would go together to lead to a main idea statement.

→ Children will listen to a group of four to five words. They will discuss possible main idea statements for the words.

→ On a flannel board, students will match pictures from a story with "who," "what," "where," and "when" words from the story.

→ After listening to a short story, children will circle three pictures, from a selection of six to eight, that best explain the main idea.

Integration of Real-Life Topics

• **Career Awareness/Work Related**
Children will identify two main characteristics/duties of the job of a class visitor (e.g., firefighter, school nurse).

• **Home and Family**
Children will tell a parent what household chores or jobs must be done before school.

• **Leisure Time**
Children will explain the object of a playground game to a group of peers.

• **Community Living**
Children will identify and discuss the main message of a morning public school announcement.

• **Emotional/Physical Health**
Children will draw a picture of their favorite part of a health-related thematic day (e.g., Healthy Heart Day, Health and Fitness Day).

Notes

_____

_____

_____

_____

_____

_____

_____

_____

_____

READING / Comprehension

Main Idea

Classroom Activities

A. After reading and/or performing a three-act skit, each student in a group of three students will share the main idea of his or her assigned act.

B. After reading a poem, children will write the key words in a cloze exercise.

C. Children will read a list of holiday activities and write a main idea statement to identify the associated holiday.

D. Given a list of untitled directions, children will formulate an appropriate title for the directions (e.g., "Building a Treehouse," "Making Cookies").

Differentiated Instruction

→ After reading, watching, and/or performing a three-act skit, each student will choose two to three words from the skit program that best explain the main idea of each act.

→ After reading a poem, children will circle the key words that relate to the main idea of the poem.

→ Children will read a list of holiday activities and draw a picture to identify the holiday.

→ Given a list of untitled directions, children will choose from a set of three pictures which picture shows the result of the directions (e.g., __ + __ + __ = cookies).

Integration of Real-Life Topics

- **Career Awareness/Work Related**
  Children will make a scrapbook page to show the main responsibilities or duties of a given career.

- **Home and Family**
  Children will discuss and/or draw/photograph the main family activities of a holiday celebration.

- **Leisure Time**
  Children will read about a vacation destination. Then they will explain the primary attractions of that destination.

- **Community Living**
  After reading about a community, children will choose a local landmark and explain its importance in that community.

- **Emotional/Physical Health**
  After reading a story (with a central character), children will choose two feeling words that describe the character's primary feelings/emotions.

Notes

_____

_____

_____

_____

_____

_____

_____

_____

_____

READING / Comprehension

Main Idea

Classroom Activities

A. Given a main idea, students will generate (orally or in writing) details that support the main idea.

B. Students will read a text in which the main idea is clear and then highlight with a marker the significant details that support the main idea.

C. Students will complete a graphic organizer that identifies the main idea and supporting details. Students will retell the story, using the graphic organizer as a guide.

D. In cooperative groups, students will complete a story map outlining the main idea of a story and its supporting details. Students will verbally explain why they chose the main idea and supporting details.

Differentiated Instruction

→ Given a main idea and flash cards with pictures, students will pick the flash card with the picture that best represents the main idea.

→ Students will read a teacher-made story printed on a poster board. Students will point to and discuss the details that support the main idea.

→ Students will finish a graphic organizer chart by choosing and inserting word cards that identify a supporting detail.

→ Working with a peer, students will draw pictures to complete a story map, identifying supporting details from the story.

Integration of Real-Life Topics

• **Career Awareness/Work Related**
After a guest speaker gives a presentation on his or her occupation, the students will write a brief paragraph summarizing two of the key responsibilities of that job.

• **Home and Family**
Students will read a story about a family and identify the main responsibilities of each family member.

• **Leisure Time**
Students will read a movie description from the newspaper and state the main idea of the movie.

• **Community Living**
On a field trip to the park, students will read the visitor's responsibilities sign and summarize its contents.

• **Emotional/Physical Health**
Students will watch a video on sports and/or physical exercise and explain the primary personal benefits of exercise.

Notes

_____

_____

_____

_____

_____

_____

_____

_____

_____

_____

_____

Main Idea

Classroom Activities

A. Students will create a poster or billboard depicting the main idea of a text without the title. Classmates will guess the selected text.

B. Using clip art, illustrations, and/or magazine photos, students will create a time line of the main story events and ideas.

C. Students will complete a graphic organizer to briefly describe the main idea(s) of the beginning, middle, and end of a selection.

D. Students will write a selection's main idea based on a set of nonsequential details from the text.

Differentiated Instruction

→ Students will draw a picture depicting the main idea of a text. Each student will present his or her picture to a small group.

→ Using teacher-made pictures of the main story events and ideas, students will create a time line.

→ Students will finish a graphic organizer using prepared pictures of a story's main idea(s). Students will place the pictures in the correct portion of the organizer.

→ Students will discuss the selection's main idea based on a set of details from the text (picture or text form).

Integration of Real-Life Topics

• **Career Awareness/Work Related**
Students will read the daily Job Chart in the classroom and tell the teacher their main responsibilities for the day.

• **Home and Family**
Students will read a text about a famous inventor and explain how the invention touches their lives.

• **Leisure Time**
Students will read lyrics to a favorite (teacher-approved) song and state the main idea and message of the song.

• **Community Living**
Students will read examples of various community rules and/or regulations (e.g., playground rules) and explain their importance.

• **Emotional/Physical Health**
Students will read a health- or sport-related magazine article and explain the primary focus of the article.

Notes

—————————————————— **Main Idea** ——————————————————

Classroom Activities

A. Students will discuss which words or phrases in a paragraph would best help generate a main idea statement.

B. Students will highlight in a text the specific paragraph that most precisely states the main idea.

C. Students will write three questions about story details to help group members generate a main idea statement.

D. Students will write a headline for a newspaper article.

Differentiated Instruction

→ Students will use prehighlighted words in a paragraph to generate a main idea statement.

→ Students will highlight the paragraph heading that shows which paragraph states the main idea.

→ Students will find a word to best answer a "who," "what," "when," or "why" question.

→ Students will find an illustration to support a headline from a newspaper article.

Integration of Real-Life Topics

- **Career Awareness/Work Related**
  Students will generate a list of careers within a specific category (e.g., technology, medicine, construction).

- **Home and Family**
  Students will interview a parent about games the parent played as a child. They will discuss the main difference between the games then and now.

- **Leisure Time**
  Students will stage a scene and act out the main idea of a favorite (teacher-approved) song.

- **Community Living**
  Students will make a poster showing the platform of a candidate in an upcoming or fictitious election.

- **Emotional/Physical Health**
  Students will discuss one of the main problems of bullying and identify a strategy for dealing with it.

Notes

_____

_____

_____

_____

_____

_____

_____

_____

_____

_____

Classifying and Categorizing

Classroom Activities

A. After a read-aloud story, the teacher will present sequence categories to the children (i.e., first, next, then, finally). Children will state a detail from the story for each category.

B. Children will read sight-word cards and place each card on a pile according to its first letter or beginning sound.

C. Children will find and cut out magazine pictures of common cafeteria foods. They will categorize each as healthy or unhealthy.

D. Children will sort a basket of books, classifying each book as fiction or nonfiction, based on the title and cover art.

Differentiated Instruction

→ Given details from a familiar story, the children will classify each detail according to its sequence in the story (beginning, middle, end).

→ Given a chart of sight words, children will identify words that fit into letter categories (e.g., find the words that start with "b").

→ Children will be shown pictures of common foods and will state if each is healthy or unhealthy.

→ Children will discuss a presorted set of books to determine if the set is fiction or nonfiction.

Integration of Real-Life Topics

• **Career Awareness/Work Related**
Children will draw a picture of a job they would like and one of a job they would not like.

• **Home and Family**
Children will place a photograph of each family member next to pictures signifying daily household chores to be done. Photos will indicate who is responsible for each chore.

• **Leisure Time**
Children will determine three activities to include on a car trip by classifying each of them as portable or not.

• **Community Living**
On a weekly trip to the recycling center, children will help to separate the recyclables and put them in the proper receptacles (e.g., paper, plastic, cardboard).

• **Emotional/Physical Health**
Children will plan a menu of four to five healthy party treats and activities to celebrate an upcoming event.

Notes

_____

_____

_____

_____

_____

_____

_____

_____

_____

_____

_____

GRADE 1

Classifying and Categorizing

Classroom Activities	Differentiated Instruction
A. Students will read a story and a nonfiction piece with the same topic. They will make a chart to categorize recalled details from each book as "real details" or "fictional details."	→ Teacher and students will read statements written on sentence strips and classify the statements as fiction or nonfiction. They will make a chart, placing each sentence strip in its category.
B. Students will read a book about two similar or related topics/groups (e.g., reptiles and birds, fruits and vegetables, Pilgrims and Indians). Students will make a class Venn diagram to show the similarities and differences between the topics.	→ Teacher and students will read a book about two similar or related topics. Teacher will display word cards related to the topic (e.g., hatch from eggs, covered with scales), and students will discuss if each is a way the topics are similar or different.
C. When learning a new set of vocabulary words, students will together classify each word as a noun, verb, or adjective, discussing their reasoning and writing each word on a classroom poster.	→ Students will discuss color-coded vocabulary words and explain why each word fits into its color category (red = nouns, green = verbs, blue = adjectives).
D. Students will read a math word problem and classify it as an addition story or a subtraction story by manipulating objects or drawing a picture to show their reasoning.	→ Students and teacher will read a math problem in which the verb is highlighted. Students will classify the word as an addition word or a subtraction word.

Integration of Real-Life Topics

- **Career Awareness/Work Related**
  Students will read about several careers and classify them (e.g., as active or nonactive, group or individual, seasonal or year-round).

- **Home and Family**
  Children will make a list of home chores and divide them among family members. They may also classify each chore as morning or evening.

- **Leisure Time**
  While cleaning a bedroom or playroom, the child will return all books to the proper section of a bookshelf that has been labeled (e.g., "Information," "Easy Readers," "Chapter Books," "Arthur Books").

- **Community Living**
  Children will read a shopping list and decide from which store each item should be purchased (e.g., grocery, pharmacy, hardware, toy store).

- **Emotional/Physical Health**
  Students will name "party drinks" and classify them as "good for a children's party" or "only for adults" (e.g., KoolAid, beer, ginger ale, champagne, milk).

Notes

_____
_____
_____
_____
_____
_____
_____
_____
_____
_____
_____

Classifying and Categorizing

Classroom Activities

A. A group of students will choose a random collection of storybooks. They will categorize the sets of books by their own criteria and explain their sorting criteria to the class.

B. Students will list all of the nouns found in a chosen story. They will classify the nouns as proper nouns or common nouns.

C. On a sticky note, each student will each write three foods for a celebration dinner. They will post their words on the board, group them (according to designated categories), and label each group.

D. Students will participate in a game of Categories. The teacher will display the category, and students will write down as many items/words/ideas that fit.

Differentiated Instruction

→ A group of students will choose a random collection of storybooks. They will categorize the sets of books using predetermined categories. They will explain why each fits its category.

→ Students will list all of the nouns found in a chosen story. They will classify the nouns as people, places, or things.

→ Students will label groups of foods (pictures and/or words) with their appropriate food group category name.

→ Students will participate in a game of Categories and as a group will generate a list of items/words/ideas that fit (by drawing, stating, pointing, writing).

Integration of Real-Life Topics

- **Career Awareness/Work Related**
  Students will classify careers according to their domain (e.g., safety, health, the arts) via pictures, word cards, charts, or graphic organizers.

- **Home and Family**
  Students will classify household responsibilities to create a family job chart for the week (e.g., cleaning jobs, meal-related jobs).

- **Leisure Time**
  Students will discuss and classify favorite leisure activities, stating if they are done individually, with a family, or with friends.

- **Community Living**
  Students will discuss and classify actions seen in the community as helpful actions or harmful actions for the community.

- **Emotional/Physical Health**
  Students will list phrases or comments that will promote healthy self-esteem in the classroom.

Notes

_____

_____

_____

_____

_____

_____

_____

_____

_____

_____

READING / Comprehension

Classifying and Categorizing

Classroom Activities

A. Students will use a graphic organizer to identify story characters and assign appropriate character attributes.

B. Students will read a newspaper article about their local community and create a time line of events in the article.

C. After reading a story about a different culture, students will create a Venn diagram of characteristics unique to that culture and characteristics that are shared by that culture and their own.

D. After reading a story with many characters, students will classify the characters in the story as major or minor and identify why they meet this criterion. They will develop a bulletin board highlighting each character.

Differentiated Instruction

→ Students will be given pictures of story characters and word cards with their attributes. Students will match the character to the attribute.

→ Students will be given cards with a series of events that happened in school. Students will place the events in order from first to last.

→ The teacher will read a story about a different culture and present the students with picture/word cards representing that culture and their own. Students will categorize the cards by culture.

→ Students will read a play with the teacher. Students will state which character is the lead role and which characters have minor roles.

Integration of Real-Life Topics

- **Career Awareness/Work Related**
  Students will read a classified ad for a particular job. Students will categorize the skills as "needed" for the job or "preferred" for the job.

- **Home and Family**
  Students will read a grocery store ad and cut out and categorize pictures for each level of the food pyramid.

- **Leisure Time**
  Students will read the local newspaper leisure section. They will classify several leisure-time activities by theme (e.g., arts, music, theater).

- **Community Living**
  The teacher and students will read an article focusing on public opinion regarding the building of a "superstore" in a community. Students will classify the arguments as pros or cons of the issue.

- **Emotional/Physical Health**
  After being presented with pictures and captions of health risks and healthy choices, students will categorize the pictures into the two types, stating their rationale for the placement of each picture.

Notes

Classifying and Categorizing

Classroom Activities

A. Students will preview vocabulary words by grouping them according to prefixes and suffixes. They will then compare their list to a partner's list and make a poster to display the words.

B. From a current novel, students will find a paragraph that best represents a story category such as plot, setting, climax, and so forth.

C. Students will develop a story chart that summarizes the major content of a story by classifying key information into story element categories.

D. After reading a biography of a famous American, students will organize specific biographical information with the headings "Who," "What," "Where," "When," and "How." They will then write a question for a class Jeopardy game, using the given categories.

Differentiated Instruction

→ Given only the meaning of a new vocabulary word (e.g., "This word means *underground*"), students will match a root word and a prefix or suffix to form the word that represents the given meaning (e.g., *subterranean*).

→ While the teacher rereads part of a story, students will identify a story detail and discuss in which story category it best fits.

→ Provided with a partially completed graphic organizer that identifies story element categories, students will complete the organizer.

→ After reading a biography of a famous American, students will make a class Jeopardy game. Students will classify given questions into the categories "Who," "What," "Where," "When," and "How."

Integration of Real-Life Topics

• **Career Awareness/Work Related**
Students will find various jobs in the "want ads" and classify them (e.g., college vs. high school education, professional vs. technical, indoor vs. outdoor).

• **Home and Family**
Students will categorize various disputes or conflicts according to strategies needed to solve them (e.g., independent, need a parent).

• **Leisure Time**
Students will classify games, activities, and sports as individual activities, partner activities, or team activities.

• **Community Living**
Students will discuss character traits (e.g., trustworthiness, respect, apathy), classifying them as "helping" or "hindering" harmonious living in various communities (home, school, neighborhood).

• **Emotional/Physical Health**
Students will identify emotional or physical problems and categorize each according to appropriate sources of help or assistance.

Notes

READING / Comprehension

Classifying and Categorizing

Classroom Activities

A. Given a list of major story element categories, students will list specific story details for each category (e.g., characters, setting, problems/solutions).

B. Students will rearrange story details on sentence strips from one set of categories to another (e.g., categories about characters, categories about sequence, categories about setting).

C. Given word cards with animal names from a science unit on animal classification, students will group the animals by class, order, or genus.

D. After reading about a major historical event, students will list given events as either major causes or outcomes of the event. They will make a chart to display for the class.

Differentiated Instruction

→ A group of students will locate specific story details for one story element category. They will post their examples as part of a class story chart.

→ Given a set of story details on sentence strips, students will categorize each as a detail about the characters, the setting, problem, solution, and so forth.

→ Given an animal classification category, students will use the Internet or an online encyclopedia to find animals that fit into the category.

→ Following a media presentation (Internet, DVD) about a major historical event, students will place prepared sentence strips in the correct category: causes or outcomes.

Integration of Real-Life Topics

• **Career Awareness/Work Related**
Students will identify jobs in the community that emphasize solving problems or resolving differences.

• **Home and Family**
Students will categorize and gather needed items for family meal preparation (e.g., ingredients, utensils).

• **Leisure Time**
Students will create a categorized list to aid in the packing and preparation for an upcoming trip or vacation.

• **Community Living**
Students will classify chosen current events as local, state, national, or international.

• **Emotional/Physical Health**
Students will discuss effective and appropriate problem-solving techniques versus ineffective and inappropriate techniques.

Notes

_____

_____

_____

_____

_____

_____

_____

_____

_____

_____

Cause and Effect

Classroom Activities

A. Children and the teacher will examine cards/posters/photos depicting familiar situations. They will discuss the "why" questions inherent in each situation and discuss the be"CAUSE" answers.

B. Children will sequence a set of picture cards that tell a story. They will discuss the reasoning for their sequence, answering "what" and "why" questions.

C. The teacher will read sentence strips of "causes." Children will discuss and draw a picture of one positive and one negative effect for each cause.

D. The teacher will read a cause-and-effect story, stopping at various "cause" points so the children can act out various effects.

Differentiated Instruction

→ When viewing and discussing pictures of familiar situations, the teacher will ask a "why" question for each situation. The children will discuss be"CAUSE" answers.

→ Given a set of partially sequenced picture cards, students will complete the sequence of the story and discuss their reasoning, including answering "what" and "why" questions.

→ The teacher will read sentence strips of causes. Children will match a picture card (that depicts the effect) with each sentence.

→ The teacher will read a cause-and-effect story, stopping at various "cause" points so the children can act out various effects. The children and teacher will discuss various effects as a group and act them out together. The teacher will guide the discussion.

Integration of Real-Life Topics

• **Career Awareness/Work Related**
Children will listen to stories about various careers. They will discuss the reasons why those jobs are helpful/important.

• **Home and Family**
Children will discuss various household chores, noting the causes and effects of doing and not doing the chores.

• **Leisure Time**
Children will participate in a safety lesson (e.g., about water, bike, bus, stranger). They will discuss and illustrate various "what if" situations.

• **Community Living**
Children will *carefully* act out a neighborhood scenario (playground, ballpark), purposely ignoring the posted rules. They will discuss the effects of ignoring the rules.

• **Emotional/Physical Health**
Children will listen to a story about a health issue (e.g., dental health, weight, physical fitness). They will match photos of various effects with their causes (e.g., cavities and soda).

Notes

_____

_____

_____

_____

_____

_____

_____

_____

_____

_____

_____

READING / Comprehension

Cause and Effect

Classroom Activities

A. Students will read a story (with instances of cause and effect) and will fill in the backward chart titled "Effect and Cause," stating what happened and why it happened.

B. After reading a story, students will identify and act out the various causes and effects in the story.

C. During a guided reading group, students will identify cause-and-effect words and phrases (e.g., *so, since, because, therefore*) from their current reading selection.

D. After reading a story, students will identify teacher-chosen phrases as either the cause or effect part of the story.

Differentiated Instruction

→ After listening to a story, students will match sentence strips of "what happened" to sentence strips of "why" from the story.

→ Students will act out preselected sets of causes and effects from a read-aloud story.

→ From a list of words and phrases, students will choose the ones that signify cause-and-effect relationships, circle them, and discuss each word or phrase.

→ After listening to a story, students will identify teacher-made pictures as depicting either a cause or an effect part of the story.

Integration of Real-Life Topics

- **Career Awareness/Work Related**
  Students will identify work habits and behaviors that would lead to positive feedback.

- **Home and Family**
  Students will discuss the effects of having and not having family meetings.

- **Leisure Time**
  Students will identify various safety rules relating to a particular sport or activity and discuss their importance.

- **Community Living**
  Students will describe a situation that would require the use of a specific community service.

- **Emotional/Physical Health**
  Students will illustrate the effects of unhealthy food on the body.

Notes

_____

_____

_____

_____

_____

_____

_____

_____

Cause and Effect

Classroom Activities

A. Using a website such as QUIA.com, children will match "cause" questions to possible effects.

B. As children read a given text, they will look for and list clue words (e.g., *if, then, since*).

C. Students will partner-read a short book and will act out cause-and-effect scenes from the story.

D. Children will read a story with a cause-and-effect structure. They will then complete a flowchart depicting each cause and its effect.

Differentiated Instruction

→ Given a set of "cause" questions on note cards or picture cards, students will match them with the corresponding effect cards.

→ As children read a given text, they will look for and highlight clue words (e.g., *if, then, since*).

→ Students will listen to a CD of a short book and will act out cause-and-effect scenes from the story.

→ Children will group-read a story with a cause-and-effect structure. They will then complete one section of a flowchart depicting a cause and an effect from the story.

Integration of Real-Life Topics

- **Career Awareness/Work Related**
  Children will read about and discuss jobs from the present and "olden days" and identify the causes of the changes they have found.

- **Home and Family**
  Children will read about and identify the effects of not maintaining, for example, one's home or property.

- **Leisure Time**
  After reading a book about friendship, students will identify positive and negative effects of peer actions. (If . . . then . . .).

- **Community Living**
  When discussing community issues, students will identify the causes of various community issues (e.g., "Why do people litter at the ballpark?").

- **Emotional/Physical Health**
  Students will identify the cause-and-effect relationships inherent in personal hygiene habits.

Notes

_____

_____

_____

_____

_____

_____

_____

_____

_____

_____

Cause and Effect

Classroom Activities

A. Students will be shown a story with which they are familiar (e.g., the "Alexander" series). Students will read the story and fill out a cause-and-effect worksheet (e.g., "Why did it happen?" "What happened?").

B. The teacher will give students captioned pictures from *Scholastic News* with cause-and-effect statements on them. Students will match the cause with the effect.

C. Students will be given a "most likely" worksheet. The students will read each sentence and circle the ending that is most likely to happen (e.g., "The temperature is 90 degrees. You will be . . .").

D. Students will read a chapter in their content-area text on rules and laws. They will then write possible effects when rules/laws are not followed.

Differentiated Instruction

→ The teacher will read a familiar story to the students. He or she will state a cause found in the story. The students will discuss and state the effect.

→ Students will read a *Scholastic News* article about current events. They are to underline any possible cause-and-effect relationships in the story.

→ Students will be given a "most likely" worksheet. The teacher will read the sentences to the students. Students are to choose one of two correct effect responses.

→ Students will be shown pictures of people breaking rules/laws. The students will state at least one possible effect of the rule/law being broken.

Integration of Real-Life Topics

- **Career Awareness/Work Related**
  Given a teacher-made story about an individual who is chronically late to work, students will write or state a possible effect of the lateness.

- **Home and Family**
  Students will write one paragraph describing their responsibilities at home. Each student will read his or her paragraph to the class. The rest of the class is to identify what would happen if the responsibilities were not met.

- **Leisure Time**
  With teacher assistance, students will read a local newspaper article about lake pollution. Students will underline cause-and-effect relationships that explain why swimming is prohibited.

- **Community Living**
  Students will take a community walk, reading safety-related signs in the community. For each sign, the students will state at least one positive effect of following the sign's message.

- **Emotional/Physical Health**
  Students will read an article that discusses good nutrition and exercise. The students will state the causes and effects of poor diet, nutrition, and exercise.

Notes

_____

_____

_____

_____

_____

_____

_____

_____

_____

_____

_____

_____

_____

_____

Cause and Effect

Classroom Activities

A. To introduce the "effect" portion of cause and effect, students will review a reading selection and list the major events that occurred in the appropriate sequence (by paragraph, page, or section).

B. For each event in a reading selection, students will identify signal words (e.g., *because, thus, since, therefore*) that provide clues to possible causes for each event.

C. The teacher will give students a list of a main character's actions, and the students will describe the story events caused by the character's action.

D. Students will discuss the idea that one event can have a single cause or multiple causes, just as multiple events can have a single cause or multiple causes. They will make a cause-and-effect chart to illustrate these various combinations.

Differentiated Instruction

→ Students will review picture cards and key vocabulary from a reading selection and will use them to identify major events that occurred in a reading selection.

→ Given a chart of cause-and-effect clue words, students will highlight those words in the text and generate a synonym for each.

→ After reading highlighted text pages, students will match the characters' actions to the events they caused.

→ The teacher will give the students a partially completed cause-and-effect chart on a SMART Board. Each student will complete part of the SMART Board chart while the rest of the class adds the answers to their personal copies.

Integration of Real-Life Topics

• **Career Awareness/Work Related**
Students will identify several behaviors that would result in successful completion of a job or task.

• **Home and Family**
Students will identify various outcomes related to storage and/or maintenance of household items (e.g., food storage, chemical storage, laundry).

• **Leisure Time**
Students will brainstorm a list of "do's" and "don'ts" in preparation for a vacation or outing.

• **Community Living**
Students will find examples of cause-and-effect relationships within selected articles or sections of a newspaper.

• **Emotional/Physical Health**
Students will act out socially appropriate actions in response to the actions or words of others.

Notes

_____

_____

_____

_____

_____

_____

_____

_____

_____

GRADE 5

Cause and Effect

Classroom Activities

A. Students will make a list of major events in a reading selection (fiction or nonfiction) and locate and match a specific causal factor for each event.

B. Students will search for and identify a cause-and-effect link or chain in their text and confirm it by identifying specific clue words (e.g., *therefore, because,* synonyms). They will display the chain as a time line or storyboard.

C. The students will develop a story "Character Chart" that lists major and minor characters, the actions of each character, and the literal or implied causes of those actions and/or characteristics. The teacher will remind students that one cause can have many effects, and one effect can have many causes.

D. After students read a fiction or nonfiction selection, the teacher will give them a list of primary and secondary story events. For each statement, the students will select a related story event, identifying it as a primary or secondary cause.

Differentiated Instruction

→ The teacher will provide the students with a set of three causal factor "answer cards" taken verbatim from a reading selection. The students will choose the one card that correctly matches the given event.

→ The teacher will give the students a set of "clue word" cards with illustrations. Students will develop a cause-and-effect link to describe events, characters, and so forth, from a story.

→ The teacher will provide the students with a partially completed "Character Chart" and answer cards. Working with a partner, students will use the cards to complete the chart.

→ Given a list of specific story events, students will discuss two to three causes of each event and categorize each as primary or secondary.

Integration of Real-Life Topics

- **Career Awareness/Work Related**
  Given a set of specific career situations (positive or negative), students will generate and discuss possible causes for each situation.

- **Home and Family**
  When discussing specific problems related to home security and safety, students will assist in the development of a class bulletin board that depicts the causes of those problems.

- **Leisure Time**
  Given a list of desirable outcomes of an activity or sport (e.g., success, improved skill, fun, safety), students will generate a list of skills and personal qualities necessary to cause the desired outcomes.

- **Community Living**
  Given a set of hypothetical emergency scenarios, students will choose the appropriate service to access to address the problem (e.g., fire, police, EMS).

- **Emotional/Physical Health**
  Given a biography of a famous athlete, students will link specific personal actions with future outcomes

(e.g., maintaining friendships, effects of prior interests on career choice).

Notes

_____

_____

_____

_____

_____

_____

_____

_____

_____

_____

WRITING

Prewriting

Content (Generating Ideas)
Organization

Writing

Expository
Narrative

Postwriting

Editing and Revising Content
Editing Mechanics

Introduction

The area of written expression often presents a major challenge to students with disabilities at the elementary school level. It is also highly correlated with concurrent problems for this group of students in the related areas of oral language, reading, and memory (as well as the written language subskills of handwriting and spelling; Graham & Harris, 2005). Many students at the elementary school level who have not been assessed as exhibiting special education needs also experience similar problems with written language skills and the process of written expression (Troia, 2005).

A written language model suggested by Polloway, Miller, and Smith (2004) outlines the many facets and related skills that are integral to the process of writing. This teachers' guide suggests several process strategies for developing skills that are essential to the writing process (Crystal, 2001; Graham & Harris, 2005; Hammill & Larsen, 2009; Lipson & Wixson, 2002; Mather, Roberts, Hammill, & Allen, 2008; Rubin, 2000). The areas of focus for written expression are as follows:

1. Prewriting—content development and organization,
2. Composition—expository and narrative, and
3. Postwriting—editing and revising for content and mechanics.

The suggested class activities, examples of instructional differentiation, and real-life applications in this section of the book focus on these three essential writing skill areas.

Content (Generating Ideas)

Classroom Activities

A. When given a topic for a class-written story, children will gather items from the classroom that represent subtopics to include in the story.

B. Following a class field trip, students will draw a picture of their favorite part of the trip. They will later write about it.

C. Before making a "My Family" book, each child will take a photograph of each person in his or her family.

D. In preparation for sending a letter to Santa, children will cut out pictures from a toy store flyer. Next to the pictures, they will write the name of each toy or item that they would like Santa to bring.

Differentiated Instruction

→ When given a topic for a class-written story and a collection of classroom items, students will choose which items will be included in the story as subtopics.

→ During a class field trip, children and adults will photograph many segments of the trip. Later, children will choose and discuss a photo that shows their favorite part of the field trip.

→ Given photographs of each person in his or her family, each child will identify each family member.

→ In preparation for sending a letter to Santa, children will circle pictures from a toy store flyer. They will "dictate" a list to the teacher.

Integration of Real-Life Topics

• **Career Awareness/Work Related**
Children will dictate to the teacher a list of words related to a given career.

• **Home and Family**
Children will draw a picture showing their choice destination for a family vacation.

• **Leisure Time**
Children will help make a list of people to invite and supplies to buy for an upcoming party.

• **Community Living**
Children will draw a picture of a favorite recreational location in their town (e.g., park, pool, amusement area), including as many details as possible.

• **Emotional/Physical Health**
Children will search (online or in magazines) for pictures that show healthy activities (emotional and physical).

Notes

_____

_____

_____

_____

_____

_____

_____

_____

WRITING / Prewriting

Content (Generating Ideas)

Classroom Activities

A. Children will make a memory collage (including drawings, photos, words, etc.) to help generate ideas about a certain event they remember.

B. Children will show the teacher a "thumbs up" if the teacher says a sentence that is truly persuasive, that is, proves a point (e.g., "It is cool" is not persuasive. "There are many places to eat at Disney World" does prove a point.). For phrases that are not persuasive, the children will suggest corrections.

C. Children will cut out a picture from a magazine or calendar. They will write a list of the things they see in the picture.

D. Students will draw four small pictures depicting the steps that show how to perform a procedure, such as brushing teeth or getting ready for bed.

Differentiated Instruction

→ Children will choose from a set of photos and word cards to help generate ideas about an event they remember.

→ Children will view a number of child-oriented commercials (e.g., for cereal). The children will say whether they would buy the product and why.

→ Children will be given a picture with a list of words under it. They will circle the words that represent things seen in the picture.

→ Given a set of pictures depicting a procedure, students will tell the teacher the proper sequence for performing the procedure.

Integration of Real-Life Topics

- **Career Awareness/Work Related**
  Children will make a list of verbs that tell what a person with a given occupation does.

- **Home and Family**
  Each child will draw and label a picture of an appropriate holiday gift for each member of his or her family.

- **Leisure Time**
  Children will bring from home photographs of a family event or vacation.

- **Community Living**
  Children will search on the Internet for photographs of symbols of the United States for a later writing activity.

- **Emotional/Physical Health**
  From a collection of food items, children will choose those that are the most healthy.

Notes

_____

_____

_____

_____

_____

_____

_____

_____

_____

Content (Generating Ideas)

Classroom Activities

A. In preparation for writing about a favorite animal or person, students will make two lists: One list will be of adjectives, and the other will be of verbs that relate to the topic.

B. Before writing about a place, students will answer a series of questions to focus their thinking (e.g., "Where will your story take place?" "What does the place look like?" "Who do you see there?").

C. Before writing a story with an assigned setting, students will think of as many words as possible that describe that setting (e.g., for setting of a birthday party: *balloons, streamers, children, presents*).

D. Given a declarative sentence such as "This is a pizza," students will generate a list of words that describe its color, shape, taste, and other characteristics.

Differentiated Instruction

→ Given an animal and a list of words, students will pick the adjectives that best describe the animal and the verbs that best relate to it.

→ Given a series of cloze sentences, students will fill in each blank to define a place they will write about (e.g., "I see . . . ," "At my place . . .").

→ Given a photograph of an assigned setting (e.g., a birthday party), students will describe the setting to a classmate.

→ Given a picture of an object with a list of words under the picture, students will circle the words that best describe the object.

Integration of Real-Life Topics

• **Career Awareness/Work Related**
Students will brainstorm a list of responsibilities of various community helpers before choosing one helper to write about.

• **Home and Family**
Given a list of household tasks, students will choose a task and list the supplies necessary to complete that task.

• **Leisure Time**
Given a closet full of a variety of sports equipment, students will choose the appropriate equipment for a given game or sport.

• **Community Living**
Students will brainstorm ideas for what should be included in a new town park and will illustrate their ideas.

• **Emotional/Physical Health**
In a weekly grocery store flyer, students will find at least one healthy food item for each of the food groups.

Notes

_____

_____

_____

_____

_____

_____

_____

_____

_____

_____

WRITING / Prewriting

Content (Generating Ideas)

Classroom Activities

A. Using an interactive story map on a website such as Read-Write-Think.org, students will generate ideas for character traits, conflicts, resolutions, and/or settings for an upcoming writing piece.

B. Given a "Character Perspective" chart, students will generate more complex ideas for a story character by answering questions such as, "What is the character's problem?" "What does the character want?" and "What will the character do to achieve his goal?"

C. Students will draw a large shape of a topic (horse, school, football). On the outline of the shape, they will write at least 10 to 12 words that describe the topic, placing commas between words in a series.

D. Given a small picture and a piece of paper, students will brainstorm about their picture. They will write down anything and everything that they can think of for 5 minutes. After 5 minutes, each student will pick three words from his or her list and write three sentences using one brainstormed word in each sentence.

Differentiated Instruction

→ In small groups, students and the teacher will generate ideas for one element of a story (such as character traits) by using an interactive story map on a website such as Read-Write-Think.org.

→ Given a "Character Perspective" chart, students will generate ideas for a character by answering a question such as, "What is the character's problem?" The teacher will record ideas on the chart, and students will act out the possibilities.

→ Given a list of adjectives, students will choose 10 to 12 words pertaining to their topic. They will write their chosen words on the outline of a shape depicting their topic.

→ Given a photograph or picture, pairs of students will write two to three adjectives, two to three nouns, and two to three verbs that relate to the picture. They will write three sentences about their picture, using one word from each category.

Integration of Real-Life Topics

• **Career Awareness/Work Related**
Using magazines, students will cut out pictures showing various careers. They will choose three pictures and brainstorm words that pertain to the careers.

• **Home and Family**
Students will generate dinner menus for the upcoming week in order to write a relevant grocery list.

• **Leisure Time**
Students will list positive reasons to participate in an upcoming event for the later purpose of writing a persuasive letter seeking permission from a parent.

• **Community Living**
Students will sketch three or four familiar locations that depict improvements in their neighborhood or town.

• **Emotional/Physical Health**
Given a picture showing the interior of a home, students will write down all of the areas in the home that may present health or safety issues.

Notes

_____
_____
_____
_____
_____
_____
_____
_____
_____
_____
_____

Content (Generating Ideas)

Classroom Activities

A. In preparation for writing a sequel or continuation of a writing project, students will review a "menu" of previous stories or topics. They will add to the list other possibilities under various categories (e.g., "Animals," "People," "Events/Places").

B. From a story or text on a chosen topic, students will highlight information with which they have a personal connection. They will create a web linking the information.

C. To expand and deepen their research base, students will develop research questions using reference sources such as personal interviews, magazine articles, bibliographies, newspapers, and Internet websites to find answers and additional information.

D. Each student will create a set of main characters and supporting characters for an upcoming writing project. (This could be created through a detailed drawing, a descriptive paragraph, or a computer-generated model.)

Differentiated Instruction

→ In preparation for writing a sequel or continuation of a writing project, small groups of students will brainstorm a specific list of topics for one category, such as "Animals" or "Events."

→ Students, in partnerships, will ask each other questions to focus their thoughts on linking personal experiences to a given text, subtopic, or story. A peer or assistant will serve as a scribe for the pair.

→ To deepen students' research base, the teacher will provide additional questions and guide the students in using reference sources such as magazine or newspaper articles, bibliographies, and so forth, to answer those questions, thus providing them with additional details and/or information.

→ Students will create a set of character traits for a given main character or supporting character for an upcoming writing project. The traits could be listed, drawn, or acted out.

Integration of Real-Life Topics

- **Career Awareness/Work Related**
  Given a list of career titles, students will compare and contrast the responsibilities, equipment, clothing, and so forth, of chosen careers.

- **Home and Family**
  Students will interview a family member to develop a personal inventory of favorite family memories (e.g., of events, pets, possessions) for that family member.

- **Leisure Time**
  Using magazines, family photos, and other items, students will make a collage depicting their favorite indoor and outdoor activities.

- **Community Living**
  In preparation for a summer reading and writing project, students will visit their local library and make a list (including specific topics and genres) of books they would like to read (with the teacher's approval).

- **Emotional/Physical Health**
  Students will develop an outline of specific topics, words, and phrases that would be used to compose different writing pieces: a letter to a friend, greeting card to a grandparent, note to a parent, or e-mail to a peer.

Notes

_____

_____

_____

_____

_____

_____

_____

_____

_____

_____

_____

_____

WRITING / Prewriting

—————— **Content (Generating Ideas)** ——————

Classroom Activities

A. Following a story, video, and/or class discussion of an historic period or event, students will identify two or three specific events in which they would like to have participated. Each student will generate a time line of his or her historical adventure.

B. Students will develop a KWL (Know, Want to know, Learn) chart (Archer & Gleason, 1989) that lists specific information related to an event. They will organize the information to help focus research on the event.

C. Given a list of questions related to a specific topic of study, the class will discuss and generate answers to the questions and categorize them into headings (e.g., "People/Traits," "Related Events/Actions," "Problems/Solutions"). These will aid in the development of a descriptive report on the topic.

D. On the website brucevanpatter.com, students will use the "Mugshots" activity to develop a main character.

Differentiated Instruction

→ After studying a given historical event, students will create a time line, highlighting specific dates, occurrences, and so forth, of the historical event. This could be written and illustrated.

→ Pairs of students will peruse a set of photographs representing a given historical event. They will use information from the photos to initiate a KWL chart.

→ The teacher will develop a set of answer cards for questions pertaining to the topic of study. Cards will be scrambled, and the students will match each answer to the correct question and category.

→ On the website brucevanpatter.com, a group of students will use the "Mugshots" activity to develop a main character for use in a group story.

Integration of Real-Life Topics

• **Career Awareness/Work Related**
Students will create a daily schedule of job responsibilities and duties for a chosen career.

• **Home and Family**
Students will create a list of ideas of how families can prevent and react to various environmental dangers and hazards (e.g., weather conditions, carbon monoxide poisoning).

• **Leisure Time**
Using a calendar as an outline, students will develop a list of various recreation/leisure activities in which their families could participate for each month.

• **Community Living**
Students will gather flyers, pamphlets, and other materials advertising a specific celebration or festival in their local community. The information will aid in the creation of a community website.

• **Emotional/Physical Health**
Prior to writing a personal improvement plan, students will maintain a log of their own daily food intake, noting healthy and unhealthy choices, fat grams, fiber, and other similar types of information.

Notes

_____

_____

_____

_____

_____

_____

_____

_____

_____

_____

_____

_____

Organization

Classroom Activities

A. Given a set of pictures depicting a familiar event (e.g., building a snowman, making dinner), children will sequence the pictures to correctly display the event.

B. Following a field trip, children will draw pictures to show three activities from the trip.

C. Given a set of school photographs (of each child in a class and several who are not), children will attach the photos to a class web to show who is in their class.

D. After discussing a given topic, the teacher will lead children in categorizing their comments/thoughts as fact, opinion, or personal experience.

Differentiated Instruction

→ Given a set of pictures depicting a familiar event (e.g., building a snowman, making dinner), children will choose one picture in the set that was included as a "mistake."

→ Following a field trip, a small group of children will draw pictures to show three activities from the trip, with each child choosing one activity to portray.

→ Using a set of school photographs (of each child in a class and several who are not), the teacher will hold up a picture. The students will give a "thumbs up" if the student in the photo is in the class and a "thumbs down" if he or she is not in the class.

→ The teacher will explain a given topic. As the topic is being discussed, the teacher will ask if the children feel the teacher's statement is fact, opinion, or personal experience.

Integration of Real-Life Topics

• **Career Awareness/Work Related**
Children will assist the teacher in organizing the relative importance of responsibilities for a particular career (e.g., firefighter, police officer) by placing pictures in either a "most important" pile or an "important" pile.

• **Home and Family**
Children will assist in the formation of a family schedule for the day, noting a logical sequence for the family's events.

• **Leisure Time**
Child will assist their parents in organizing what they would like to do on each day of a family vacation.

• **Community Living**
After a community walk, children will draw a picture of at least three things they saw in the community and categorize each as a person, place, or thing.

• **Emotional/Physical Health**
Children will categorize pictures of grocery items according to food groups and/or healthy and unhealthy foods.

Notes

_____

_____

_____

_____

_____

_____

_____

_____

_____

_____

WRITING / Prewriting

Organization

Classroom Activities

A. The teacher and students will construct a "hamburger" poster to show the parts of a story. (The buns are the beginning and the end. The burger and toppings are details of the story.) Children will label and discuss each part.

B. After brainstorming about a variety of places in a shopping mall, students will write each place under the heading that fits best (e.g., "Clothing," "Food," "Entertainment").

C. Students will review teacher-made word webs and evaluate each part of the web for its relevance to the given topic, eliminating any words and phrases that do not fit.

D. After generating a list and making word/phrase cards of procedures and ingredients for a given recipe, students will begin to organize the recipe by sequencing the procedural cards and categorizing the ingredients cards.

Differentiated Instruction

→ Groups of students will retell a story from beginning to end, pointing to a "hamburger" poster to identify the part of the story being retold.

→ After reading a story about shopping, the teacher will ask questions about shopping, leading the children in discussing the various places and purposes for shopping.

→ The teacher will hold up a sentence strip related to a given topic. Students will hold up a "yes" card if it is relevant to the topic and a "no" card if it is not relevant.

→ After the teacher reads aloud from a book that contains a basic recipe, the students will list the ingredients for the recipe to make a grocery list.

Integration of Real-Life Topics

- **Career Awareness/Work Related**
  Using words, sentence strips, or pictures, students will categorize equipment used in several careers as "Essential" or "Nonessential."

- **Home and Family**
  Children will generate a chart showing the categories used for a family grocery list.

- **Leisure Time**
  Children will assist their parents in organizing what clothes to bring on a family vacation, taking into account location, temperature, and other factors.

- **Community Living**
  The class will take a community-based field trip. As a class, they will plan their day according to what they would like to do before and after lunch.

- **Emotional/Physical Health**
  Children will draw pictures to show a daily schedule for exercise and tell what they would do for exercise on a particular day.

Notes

_____

_____

_____

_____

_____

_____

_____

_____

_____

_____

Organization

Classroom Activities

A. The teacher will model how to create a semantic map. The class will use words, phrases, topics, and so forth, from a previous lesson to fill out the semantic map.

B. Each student will be given a five- to six-sentence story cut apart into individual sentence strips. The student will reconstruct the story in an order that makes sense and/or follows a given format.

C. Students will each generate a list of three to five character attributes to include in a story outline.

D. After researching a given topic, students will rank-order each fact or idea according to its importance or relevance by making a list on a large chart.

Differentiated Instruction

→ The teacher will show students a partially completed semantic map focusing on a teacher-selected topic. The students will complete the map by choosing the correct word/phrase cards and placing them on the map.

→ Given three to five story pictures, students will order the pictures from first to last and tell the story in their own words.

→ From a teacher-generated list, students will pick three to five relevant character attributes to include in a story outline.

→ After a teacher presentation on a given topic, the teacher will present sentence strips of facts, and the students will categorize the strips as relevant or not relevant.

Integration of Real-Life Topics

• **Career Awareness/Work Related**
Given a list of job responsibilities, students will discuss what they like/do not like about the job.

• **Home and Family**
Given a list of family chores, children will assist in assigning tasks to each family member.

• **Leisure Time**
Given a local weather forecast and a list of clothing items, children will choose the most appropriate items for a current outdoor activity.

• **Community Living**
When shown a DVD of various forms of public transportation, students will place them into one of two categories: "Available in My Community" or "Not Available in My Community."

• **Emotional/Physical Health**
Students will be shown various pictures of health-related scenarios. Students will categorize the pictures as a "Health Risk" or "Not a Health Risk."

Notes

WRITING / Prewriting

Organization

Classroom Activities	Differentiated Instruction
A. Using an interactive website such as teach-nology.com or recipes4success.com, students will complete a graphic organizer.	→ Working in pairs, students will use a relevant website to help them finish a partially completed graphic organizer.
B. After reading a text chapter on a given topic, students will take brief notes, organizing them in a semantic map or a series of semantic maps.	→ After reading a text chapter together as a class, small groups will highlight the key points in the chapter and then decide which points are most important.
C. Each student will write two to four sentences about one aspect of a current topic of study (e.g., one part of a life cycle, weather in the location being studied, food in the location being studied). As a class, students will organize and sequence their sentences to generate a cohesive and complete report.	→ In groups, students will sequence a list of ideas about a current topic of study. As a class, they will generate a story or report using the sequenced ideas.
D. Students will illustrate a representation of their dream house (or vacation, outfit, or meal). They will later write about their dream subject, including details depicted in their picture.	→ Students will draw a picture of their dream house (or vacation, outfit, or meal). They will discuss the most essential component(s) of their dream item.

Integration of Real-Life Topics

- **Career Awareness/Work Related**
  Given a particular career and a variety of work habits, students will organize the work habits as "Acceptable" or "Not Acceptable."

- **Home and Family**
  Given a room in the house, the students will arrange furniture and equipment to make the best use of the space.

- **Leisure Time**
  Given a selection of outdoor activities, students will rank-order the activities from favorite to least favorite.

- **Community Living**
  Working in groups, students will discuss the voting process. They will then make a time line depicting the various events in an election.

- **Emotional/Physical Health**
  Given an emergency situation (e.g., a fire), students will order pictures as to what they should do first, second, third, and so forth.

Notes

_____

_____

_____

_____

_____

_____

_____

_____

_____

_____

_____

WRITING / Prewriting

Organization

Classroom Activities

A. Given a teacher-generated "menu" of famous Americans, students will select a person and make a list of questions they'd like to be answered through research.

B. Students will develop a list of a variety of appropriate research sources and rank-order their relevance to the chosen topic.

C. Using a website such as muralmosaic.com, students will click on an individual panel and brainstorm a list of words to describe the picture.

D. Students will develop a story plot outline based on a character, setting, and problem provided by the teacher.

Differentiated Instruction

→ With a partner (who chose the same topic), each child will discuss the reasons for their selection and will list information that they already know about the topic.

→ A small group of students will brainstorm a list of research sources that they have previously used. They will discuss the relative usefulness of each source.

→ Using a website such as muralmosaic.com, students will click on an individual mosaic panel and dictate words to describe the picture.

→ Given a series of questions with answers, students will group them according to common features (e.g., characters, setting, problem).

Integration of Real-Life Topics

- **Career Awareness/Work Related**
  Students will list occupations involved in various levels of conflict resolution.

- **Home and Family**
  Students will identify a location for a family vacation and will develop a set of questions to help familiarize themselves with the destination. They will identify a reference source that could provide answers.

- **Leisure Time**
  Students will categorize family activities according to family preferences (e.g., entire family vs. individual preferences).

- **Community Living**
  Students will develop an informational chart on major community organizations. They will outline specific information for each organization (e.g., category, contact person, location).

- **Emotional/Physical Health**
  Students will interview a classmate and list his or her personal accomplishments.

Notes

_____

_____

_____

_____

_____

_____

_____

_____

_____

_____

_____

WRITING / Prewriting

Organization

Classroom Activities	Differentiated Instruction
A. The teacher will give students category headings under which they will list specific questions to focus their research (e.g., "People/Traits," "Related Events and Actions," "Problems/Solutions").	→ Given category headings ("People/Traits," "Related Events and Actions," "Problems/Solutions") and factual information obtained from research, small groups of students will categorize each fact to aid in the illustration of each event (or person).
B. Using a website such as MakeBeliefsComix.com, students will create a comic strip to later be turned into a full story.	→ Using a website such as MakeBeliefsComix.com, the class will create a comic strip, followed by a corresponding class story.
C. Given menus of characters, settings, problems, and solutions, students will choose one item from each category to create a tentative story map.	→ Given a character, setting, and problem/solution, students will organize the elements into a tentative story map.
D. Provided with details about two factual events, students will organize the details into a Venn diagram before writing a "Compare and Contrast" essay.	→ Given details of two factual events, students will use a SMART Board or a mimeo board to manipulate the events to create a Venn diagram showing similarities and differences.

Integration of Real-Life Topics

- **Career Awareness/Work Related**
  Given a list of occupations that interest them, each student will choose one and compare and contrast it with the same job, or a similar one, from a previous historical time period.

- **Home and Family**
  Given a collection of dated and identified family photos, students will develop an outline of a family tree.

- **Leisure Time**
  Working from a list of recreational and camping activities, students will devise a schedule to accommodate time constraints, personal interests, and physical space.

- **Community Living**
  Using the major headings found in the local Yellow Pages of the phone book, students will construct an outline of services that their families access.

- **Emotional/Physical Health**
  Students will organize an outline of self-evaluative questions. They will use this outline to focus and chart progress toward improvement in a personal area such as scholastic performance, social interactions, or personal appearance.

Notes

_____

_____

_____

_____

_____

_____

_____

_____

_____

_____

_____

_____

_____

Expository

Classroom Activities

A. Children will sequence a set of pictures depicting a life cycle (of an animal or plant) and will write one relevant word for each picture.

B. Together as a class, children will formulate a list of words, phrases, and sentences describing appropriate classroom behavior. The teacher will serve as guide and scribe.

C. Children will each write a recipe, including an ingredient list and directions, for a favorite or funny food.

D. Children will write an "All About Me" or other booklet by filling in blank spaces in a teacher-made booklet.

Differentiated Instruction

→ Given a set of sequenced pictures depicting a life cycle (of an animal or a plant), children will write one word relevant to each picture.

→ As the teacher and an assistant read sentence strips describing examples of both appropriate and inappropriate classroom behaviors, children will choose the sentences that show appropriate behavior and tape them together to make a complete list.

→ After listening to a story that tells how to make a favorite food, children will write the recipe for preparing that food.

→ Using a partially prepared PowerPoint presentation, children will fill in blank spaces to complete the information and create an "All About Me" or other presentation.

Integration of Real-Life Topics

- **Career Awareness/Work Related**
  Children will draw a picture of their favorite classroom job and write a sentence identifying it.

- **Home and Family**
  Children will fill in necessary information on invitations to an upcoming birthday party.

- **Leisure Time**
  Children will write a letter to a grandparent, asking to visit and telling one thing they would like to do at the grandparent's house.

- **Community Living**
  Children will create a sign that includes pictures and relevant informational words and phrases for an upcoming sale (e.g., lemonade, bake).

- **Emotional/Physical Health**
  Children will choose one family member and write a short list of words or phrases that tell how that person makes them feel.

Notes

_____

_____

_____

_____

_____

_____

_____

_____

_____

WRITING

Expository

WRITING

Classroom Activities	Differentiated Instruction

Classroom Activities

A. Given a photograph without people in it, children will write sentences beginning with "the" to describe the picture (e.g., "The tree is very tall").

B. After discussing a favorite birthday gift, children will write a short paragraph telling why they like the gift.

C. Following a field trip, children will write a paragraph describing the trip in sequence.

D. Children will write and illustrate their own life "history," including one significant event from each year.

Differentiated Instruction

→ Given a photograph without people in it and a list of words related to the picture, children will write sentences beginning with "the" to tell about the picture (e.g., "The tree is very tall").

→ After discussing a favorite birthday gift, children will use an overhead projector, SMART Board, or chart paper to craft a group paragraph about the gift.

→ Following a field trip and given a schedule of the day, children will write a paragraph describing the trip in sequence.

→ After discussing their life "history," children will be videotaped showing and explaining pictures of one significant event from each year. They will show one previously written word for each picture.

Integration of Real-Life Topics

- **Career Awareness/Work Related**
  Following a presentation by a class visitor on Career Day, children will write about and illustrate one responsibility that person has.

- **Home and Family**
  Before a weekend or vacation, children will write a list of activities to use when they begin to get bored at home.

- **Leisure Time**
  Children will choose a favorite team sport or group activity and will write three reasons they enjoy it.

- **Community Living**
  Children will compose a group or individual thank-you letter to a worker in their school, acknowledging the jobs that person performs.

- **Emotional/Physical Health/Responsibilities**
  At the end of a day, at home or at school, children will write a journal entry noting their day's accomplishments.

Notes

_____

_____

_____

_____

_____

_____

_____

_____

_____

_____

Expository

Classroom Activities

A Children will write the steps for "building" a sandwich as the teacher demonstrates each step. They will then read each step, and one student will "build" the sandwich, following the directions being read.

B. Given a topic sentence and a concluding sentence, students will complete a paragraph by adding the relevant details and explanations for the middle of the paragraph.

C. After visiting a nursing home during a holiday, students will write about and illustrate their favorite part(s) of the visit.

D. Students will describe, in writing, a pet they know well, including the main characteristics of the pet (e.g., color, size, food).

Differentiated Instruction

→ The teacher will demonstrate the steps in "building" a sandwich and hold up word cards that match each step. Students will write each step of the process in sequence after using the word cards as cues.

→ Given a series of details and explanations, students will write a topic sentence and a concluding sentence for the details.

→ After visiting a nursing home during a holiday, students will draw at least one illustration representing their trip and write a sentence that describes their illustration.

→ When shown a picture of an animal, students will write one sentence for each major characteristic as identified by the teacher (e.g., "What is the size of the animal?").

Integration of Real-Life Topics

• **Career Awareness/Work Related**
Students will choose a job they would not like to have and will write a description of the job and their reasons for not wanting it.

• **Home and Family**
Students will write a letter explaining a home chore and how much allowance they think it warrants. They will give three reasons for the amount they think they should receive.

• **Leisure Time**
After watching a community theater production, students will write a paragraph explaining the show to someone who was not at the production.

• **Community Living**
Following a day of Earth Day activities, students will write a short paragraph that describes the day for inclusion in the class newsletter.

• **Emotional/Physical Health/Responsibilities**
Students will write a letter to the local government agency describing a current environmental concern found in the community.

Notes

_____

_____

_____

_____

_____

_____

_____

_____

_____

_____

_____

WRITING

GRADE 3

Expository

Classroom Activities

A. After the teacher suggests a topic of interest to the students (e.g., "Should snack time be banned in school?"), the students will write a letter to the principal citing their reasons for saying yes or no.

B. After a visit to a museum, students will write about the exhibit they liked best and why.

C. After listening to a piece of classical music and a piece from another genre of music, students will write about the feelings they felt while listening to each.

D. While making slime, students will write a descriptive paragraph of its major properties (e.g., color, texture).

Differentiated Instruction

→ After the teacher suggests a topic of interest to the students (e.g., "Why we should not have school tomorrow") and lists possible details, students will write three sentences in favor of or against the proposal.

→ After a visit to a museum, the teacher will show students pictures of various exhibits in the museum. They will select one picture and write why they liked that display.

→ After listening to a piece of music, students will write about why they liked or disliked the piece.

→ While making slime, students will write at least three sentences that describe how the slime felt, smelled, and so forth, using the five senses as cues.

Integration of Real-Life Topics

• **Career Awareness/Work Related**
When studying about a different country or continent, students will write about a career that is not generally found in the United States.

• **Home and Family**
Students will write a paragraph describing a celebration or holiday unique to a particular area, country, or culture.

• **Leisure Time**
Following a recreational movie presentation, students will write a review of the movie to persuade someone else to see it.

• **Community Living**
Students will write a descriptive menu for a real or fictitious restaurant.

• **Emotional/Physical Health/Responsibilities**
Students will write a personal letter to someone who is in need of encouragement.

Notes

_____

WRITING

Expository

Classroom Activities

A. After discussing a prominent school or community problem(s), students will select a specific topic and develop a paragraph that describes a solution for or an improvement in the problem or situation.

B. Using a completed graphic organizer, children will create a time line of their lives and then use the time line to draft an autobiography.

C. After reading a humorous back-to-school story, students will explain a personal connection to the story (e.g., similar events, emotions).

D. Students will write a summary of a persuasive presentation that they will make to the class. Included will be specific support to substantiate their proposal or views.

Differentiated Instruction

→ Groups of students will discuss a specific school problem and will jointly develop sentences that describe a solution for or an improvement in the problem situation.

→ Using a completed time line, children will select three events from their lives and describe each event.

→ After reading a humorous back-to-school story, students will help generate a list of questions to be discussed and choose one question to answer in writing.

→ Provided with relevant visual outlines (webs/maps), pairs of students will develop a poster and an accompanying paragraph that explains their views on the given subject.

Integration of Real-Life Topics

- **Career Awareness/Work Related**
  Students will write a paragraph describing in priority order the three most important jobs/duties/responsibilities performed by a family member.

- **Home and Family**
  Students will write a thank-you note to a family member (parent, sibling, other) expressing why they appreciated a previous gift or assistance with a task.

- **Leisure Time**
  Students will develop a series of journal entries (daily for 1 week) describing favorite free-time activities, both in school and at home, and will include a specific reason why an activity was chosen.

- **Community Living**
  Students will develop an ad for a neighborhood yard sale that provides information regarding location, date, time, and specific highlights of items for sale.

- **Emotional/Physical Health**
  Students will develop a poster with a persuasive caption describing specific tips and related reasons for practicing safe habits when bicycling, rollerblading, or performing other outdoor activities.

Notes

WRITING

Expository

Classroom Activities

A. Students will complete an independent, free-choice book report containing the following information: (a) title and author and (b) a summary consisting of three to five sentences describing the book's plot, setting, and main characters.

B. Students will review videotapes, audiotapes, or pictures related to a book that they have selected and develop the script for an advertisement for the book.

C. After reading a selected book, going on a field trip, or watching a movie and related media materials, students will develop a questionnaire about their book or experience that is designed to gather their classmates' opinions.

D. Students will develop a paragraph describing the most interesting character or event within a book, including supporting details such as a personal account of a similar experience.

Differentiated Instruction

→ After participating in a language-experience activity focusing on a book summary, students will write an organized content outline and then an initial draft of a summary.

→ Pairs of students will locate or draw pictures related to a chosen story. They will use the pictures to make a poster that advertises the book.

→ With assistance from a teacher or aide, students will describe a personal event or experience that holds a particular level of interest to them. They will write two to three questions to pose to their peers after the peers have read about the event.

→ Groups of students will discuss various personal connections to stories they have read. Students will assist in the development of sentences describing (a) similar experiences they have encountered, (b) similar people they have met, or (c) similar dialogue or reactions to those of the story's characters.

Integration of Real-Life Topics

• **Career Awareness/Work Related**
Students will write a short letter to a community business or professional in which they request information on a specific job that was identified within a book they have read.

• **Home and Family**
Through a series of journal entries, students will describe specific pictures from a family photo album.

• **Leisure Time**
Students will develop a paragraph that compares the recreational activities available to children in a story with leisure-time opportunities available to them and their classmates.

• **Community Living**
Students will write an essay in which they describe and offer details about a person from the community who has had an impact on their lives.

• **Emotional/Physical Health**
Students will develop one or two paragraphs related to a dangerous or questionable health/personal

action in a previously read book. They will discuss possible actions to avoid or modify these behaviors.

Notes

_____

WRITING

Narrative

Classroom Activities

A. After participating in a reading of a predictable story, such as *Brown Bear, Brown Bear, What Do You See?* by Bill Martin, Jr., children will complete and illustrate a page for a class book (e.g., "Susie, Susie, what do you see? I see a . . .").

B. Children will caption and illustrate an "All About Me" book in which they include one page each for "Me," "My Family," "My Pets," and "My House."

C. Using a shared writing format, children will take part in the creation of a class story, with each child doing some of the actual writing commensurate with his or her ability level.

D. Upon returning from a field trip, children will write and illustrate a journal entry describing the trip.

Differentiated Instruction

→ After participating in a reading of a predictable story, such as *Brown Bear, Brown Bear, What Do You See?* by Bill Martin, Jr., each child will illustrate a page for a class book.

→ With a "Kinderpal" from third or fourth grade, children will caption and illustrate an "All About Me" book in which they include one page each for "Me," "My Family," "My Pets," and "My House."

→ Children will take part in the creation of a class story by discussing and dictating words, phrases, and sentences to the teacher.

→ Upon returning from a field trip, pairs of children will draw a picture of a scene from the trip and write any words they think go with the picture.

Integration of Real-Life Topics

• **Career Awareness/Work Related**
After choosing a favorite job, students will find or draw a picture showing that job and include a message in a word bubble.

• **Home and Family**
Using alphabet magnets on the home refrigerator, children will find letters to write the names of people and pets in the home.

• **Leisure Time**
Children will sequence photos of their family vacation and dictate a sentence about each photo to document their vacation.

• **Community Living**
Children will create a poster to promote an upcoming community festival. Captions about festival goers will be included.

• **Emotional/Physical Health**
Given a set of photographs clearly depicting a variety of emotions, children will match words to each photo and tell about a time when they felt that emotion.

Notes

_____

_____

_____

_____

_____

_____

_____

_____

_____

_____

WRITING

Narrative

Classroom Activities

A. Using a list of words and phrases, children will describe, in writing, a recent event. The event will be described using the first-person voice.

B. Children will write a story by using a story map that is focused on a given main idea. The story should contain all elements from the story map.

C. After choosing a favorite animal and listing its characteristics, children will write a story as if they were the animal.

D. After reading a story about an adventure, children will write about a time they had an adventure.

Differentiated Instruction

→ Given a set of completed sentence strips that describe a recent event, children will glue them in the correct order to tell "the story" of the event.

→ In a small, teacher-guided group, children will each create a story, following the elements of a previously made story map that includes pictures.

→ After listening to a short story about a fictional animal, children will choose a different animal and write a story following the same story format and elements as the original story.

→ After reading a story about an adventure and using a series of pictures depicting the adventure, children will write a story following the "plot" shown in the pictures.

Integration of Real-Life Topics

- **Career Awareness/Work Related**
Children will write a story on "A Day in the Life of a . . . ." They will imagine that they have a particular career and will tell the story of a typical day.

- **Home and Family**
Children will write a letter to a family member in which they describe their dog or cat (or a pet of a friend or neighbor) and dictate the letter into a digital recorder for the family member to listen to.

- **Leisure Time**
Children will choose a vacation destination and write a journal entry telling what they would do if they went there.

- **Community Living**
Children will describe the process of recycling by telling what would happen to them if they were a bottle or can to be recycled.

- **Emotional/Physical Health**
Children will write a story depicting a bullying situation. They will then revise it or write another story showing "better" social interactions.

Notes

WRITING

Narrative

Classroom Activities

A. After reading a nonfiction text about an animal, children will write a fictional story about the animal using some of the facts from the nonfiction text.

B. After visiting a local historic site, children will write a journal entry as if they were part of the historic site and its story.

C. Children will write a creative story following an "If I were a . . ." format.

D. Children will write a friendly letter to a relative explaining a recent art or science project they enjoyed.

Differentiated Instruction

→ After the teacher reads a nonfiction text about an animal to the children, they will dictate a fictional story about the animal in which they use at least three facts from the nonfiction text.

→ After visiting a local historic site, children will draw a picture of what they would see if they were part of the historic site and its story. They will then write a description of their picture.

→ Children will fill in the blanks of a pre-made creative story that follows the "If I were a . . ." format.

→ Given a set of photographs taken during a recent art or science project, students will write a friendly letter explaining the project.

Integration of Real-Life Topics

- **Career Awareness/Work Related**
  Students will write a list of at least three skills required for a particular job (e.g., vet). They will write a narrative describing in detail each task for one of the skills.

- **Home and Family**
  Students will write a story about an imaginary family pet they wish they could have.

- **Leisure Time**
  Students will write and illustrate a journal entry about their favorite sports team's participation in the league championship.

- **Community Living**
  Students will make a photo album, with captions, of a recent visit to a nursing home or hospital.

- **Emotional/Physical Health**
  Students will write a personal letter of admiration or appreciation to a friend who has recently done a good deed or achieved a goal.

Notes

_____
_____
_____
_____
_____
_____
_____
_____
_____
_____

WRITING

Narrative

WRITING

Classroom Activities

A. Given a comic strip with several blank panels, students will complete each panel with text and illustrations.

B. After having read and discussed several "Anansi stories," children will write an ending to a new Anansi story.

C. While conducting a lesson on immigration, the teacher will show students a photo of a group of immigrants. They will choose one person and write a journal entry describing the person's thoughts at that moment.

D. Children will write a science fiction story after being given a prompt such as, "Imagine that . . . you arrive at school to find an alien at the teacher's desk" or "While you are reading a favorite story, one of the characters jumps out of the book."

Differentiated Instruction

→ Given a comic strip with illustrations that are out of sequence, students will sequence the appropriate illustrations and provide the text in the form of sentences or captions.

→ After having read and discussed several "Anansi stories," children will select from several choices an ending to best fit a new Anansi story. They will then write the ending.

→ When shown a picture of an immigrant, the students will use words from a teacher-made word bank to write what that person might be feeling/thinking.

→ Children will collectively dictate a science fiction story after being given a prompt such as, "Imagine that you arrive at school to find an alien at your desk." Each child will contribute one sentence to the story.

Integration of Real-Life Topics

- **Career Awareness/Work Related**
  Imagining that they are one of their parents, students will tell a first-hand account of an unusual event at their workplace.

- **Home and Family**
  After realizing that no one will be coming to a planned event (e.g., birthday party), students will describe their feelings and reactions.

- **Leisure Time**
  After choosing a favorite book or story from their summer, children will create an alternate ending to the book or story.

- **Community Living**
  Following an annual community festival or event, children will describe their favorite part of the event for an article in the community newsletter.

- **Emotional/Physical Health**
  Provided with the scenario of a national health epidemic (real or imaginary), students will describe their opinion as to how the epidemic could have been avoided.

Notes

_____

_____

_____

_____

_____

_____

_____

_____

_____

_____

_____

Narrative

Classroom Activities

A. Based on Internet research about extreme emergencies and disasters, students will imagine that they are reporters for a newspaper, magazine, or other media outlet. They will develop a detailed description of an event from an eyewitness perspective.

B. Students will develop a narrative describing both the short-term and long-term responses to a hypothetical situation.

C. The class will develop a series of short letters to local officials in which they discuss a local community controversy. The letters will request suggestions for addressing the controversy.

D. Each student will develop a poster accompanied by a detailed narrative of one aspect of an event or situation. Each student's product will be compiled into a description of the entire event.

Differentiated Instruction

→ After reading about a local disaster and using an outline that contains key words and phrases, pairs of students will develop an imaginary eyewitness account of an extreme emergency or disaster.

→ Given a chart displaying the short-term and long-term responses to a hypothetical situation, pairs of students will organize the information and share it with the class. The class will then develop a narrative describing the situations.

→ Given a completed generic letter to a local official that describes a community issue, students will modify the letter to fit a chosen issue and request assistance from the official.

→ Following a teacher demonstration and given a teacher-developed checklist, students will develop a poster and descriptive narrative of a given event.

Integration of Real-Life Topics

- **Career Awareness/Work Related**
  Given the title of a fictitious public service career (e.g., flagpole polisher), students will describe the various roles and responsibilities related to that career.

- **Home and Family**
  Given a specific event or situation from their past, students will describe the sequence of events, including relevant details.

- **Leisure Time**
  Students will describe—in the form of a story—ways that they would entertain themselves without any modern conveniences.

- **Community Living**
  Students will describe what the people in their neighborhood would have done during an historical event (e.g., Boston Tea Party).

- **Emotional/Physical Health**
  Students will write a journal entry describing a time when they either gave or received first aid or assistance.

Notes

_____

_____

_____

_____

_____

_____

_____

_____

_____

_____

_____

WRITING

Narrative

Classroom Activities

A. Based on a synthesis of content from a number of journal entries related to a specific event, students will develop a personal narrative that describes the event as a whole.

B. Given specific criteria to include, students will develop an initial draft of a narrative, being sure to include each criterion.

C. Students will compare and contrast two previously completed narratives that describe a similar event. They will then identify their preferred version and explain why.

D. Students will develop a narrative of a recent event that they enjoyed. They will describe the event to someone in the form of a postcard or letter.

Differentiated Instruction

→ Given a visual web of ideas and a corresponding vocabulary list, students will write a draft of a personal narrative.

→ After a teacher demonstration containing specific examples and visual cues (e.g., pictures, diagrams, words), students will develop an initial draft of their narrative.

→ Given visual outlines of two similar events, students will write captions for the event that they prefer.

→ Pairs of students will develop an enlarged example of a postcard or letter for a class presentation.

Integration of Real-Life Topics

• **Career Awareness/Work Related**
Given a list of specific job titles and related duties/responsibilities, students will write a narrative describing a chosen job as if they held that job.

• **Home and Family**
Students will choose a family holiday celebration and will describe their own family's activities during the celebration.

• **Leisure Time**
Students will develop an invitation letter for an upcoming event. The invitation will describe a variety of tentative outdoor and indoor activities that are being planned.

• **Community Living**
Students will select a local community and research its history. They will choose an event they would have liked to take part in and will describe it as if they were there.

• **Emotional/Physical Health**
Students will write a personal narrative that describes an example of a time they were proud of their own actions and/or reactions.

Notes

_____

_____

_____

_____

_____

_____

_____

_____

_____

_____

_____

_____

WRITING

Editing and Revising Content

Classroom Activities

A. Given a set of pictures that depicts a short story but also includes several irrelevant pictures, students will put an "X" on the pictures that do not belong.

B. Children and the teacher will discuss a list of words and phrases that describe a given object. The teacher will encourage recognition of specific and descriptive word choices.

C. The teacher will read aloud a class-made chart of a recipe. Children will discuss and revise, if necessary, the sequence of the steps and the ingredients.

D. Given a long list of a large variety of school supplies, the class will shorten the list by deciding which supplies are necessities.

Differentiated Instruction

→ Given a set of pictures depicting a common theme (e.g., plants, animals, shapes), children will eliminate any pictures that do not belong in the set.

→ When shown a picture and two teacher-made word cards, students will identify the most descriptive word.

→ While the teacher reads aloud a recipe or other directions, children will signal the teacher when they hear something out of context.

→ Given word cards of a previously made list of school supplies, children will move each card to show if it is a necessity or an "extra."

Integration of Real-Life Topics

• **Career Awareness/Work Related**
Following several visits from community workers and several Language Experience writings, children will work together to add another detail to a previously written job description.

• **Home and Family**
After dictating a story about their family's holiday traditions, children will listen to their stories and then write a title and draw a cover picture for each story.

• **Leisure Time**
After listing the possible ingredients to make a favorite snack, children will make the snack and then revise the list to reflect the actual ingredients by eliminating some and adding others.

• **Community Living**
After a sale of Girl Scout cookies, 4H cookies, or Cub Scout popcorn, students will help tally and record the final order, being sure to double-check it for accuracy.

• **Emotional/Physical Health**
After dictating a list of foods they ate in a day, students will revise the list to reflect a healthier diet and take the list home to share with their families.

Notes

_____

_____

_____

_____

_____

_____

_____

_____

_____

_____

Editing and Revising Content

Classroom Activities

A. Using previously made lists of favorite words (e.g., "Funny Words," "Tasty Words," "Strange Words"), children will either circle favorite words in their writing or will change words to "better" ones.

B. After writing a description of a familiar "mystery object," students will read the description to classmates. The classmates will then draw the object by following the details in the description.

C. In a postwriting peer conference, students will underline the first word of each sentence, noting and replacing any too frequently used words.

D. Using a class-written narrative story, the class will reread the piece and find two or three appropriate places to insert dialogue.

Differentiated Instruction

→ Children will listen to each other's paragraphs and signal when they hear a word from a previously made word list (e.g., "Funny Words," "Tasty Words," "Strange Words").

→ After writing a description of a familiar "mystery object," students will read the paragraph to classmates and display two objects. Classmates will decide which object is being described.

→ In a postwriting conference, with a small group of peers, children will read their writing and tally how many times chosen words are used.

→ Given two class-written narrative stories, children will reread them and decide which story would benefit from adding dialogue.

Integration of Real-Life Topics

- **Career Awareness/Work Related**
  Given a classroom schedule, children will reread and revise it to provide time for a desired or needed activity.

- **Home and Family**
  After writing a paragraph about a messy room, children will then clean their room and revise the paragraph to reflect the cleaning improvements.

- **Leisure Time**
  After writing a contract stating pet care or other household responsibilities, the children will attempt to perform all of the jobs for 1 week. They will then revisit the contract and revise it to reflect a more realistic number of responsibilities.

- **Community Living**
  After writing a birthday gift list for a classmate's birthday party, children will visit the local store to find out which items are available and will be within a given price range. They will revise their list to make a final gift choice.

- **Emotional/Physical Health**
  After writing about a hypothetical playground situation, students will discuss the event and then revise their writing to reflect a different outcome, positive or negative.

Notes

_____

_____

_____

_____

_____

_____

_____

_____

_____

_____

_____

_____

_____

_____

_____

_____

WRITING / Postwriting

Editing and Revising Content

Classroom Activities

A. After the students write personal persuasive paragraphs, the teacher will read aloud the paragraphs without revealing the author. The class will guess the author based on the "voice" in the paragraph.

B. Given a story written by the class, students will independently read the story and replace any mundane adjectives with more vibrant ones.

C. After writing a descriptive paragraph, students will reread their work, noting where more detail is needed. They will add these details.

D. After writing an article for the class newsletter, students will edit each other's work for word choice by using a beginner's thesaurus to find stronger words.

Differentiated Instruction

→ A small group of students will read two personal persuasive paragraphs. They will discuss which one shows more personality.

→ Given a teacher-written story, students (in pairs) will read the story and edit it for word choice by circling adjectives that are mundane.

→ After writing a descriptive paragraph, students will read their writing to a small group of peers. The group will indicate points that are too vague.

→ Given an article (with a blank in each sentence) from a class newsletter, students will choose from three choices a word that best completes the sentence, strengthening word choice and avoiding repetitive words and phrases.

Integration of Real-Life Topics

• **Career Awareness/Work Related**
Given a paragraph describing a school job and containing irrelevant sentences, students will find and omit the irrelevant sentences.

• **Home and Family**
Given a vacation packing list from the summer, children will revise the list for a vacation in a different season or location.

• **Leisure Time**
While reading a favorite chapter book, students will tally the number of times descriptive adjectives were used in one chapter.

• **Community Living**
Students will update a list of neighborhood services to make it current. The list will be included in a "Welcome Wagon" package for new neighbors.

• **Emotional/Physical Health**
Given a mock magazine article that describes an unhealthy lifestyle, children will revise it to reflect healthy choices.

Notes

_____

_____

_____

_____

_____

_____

_____

_____

_____

WRITING / Postwriting

Editing and Revising Content

Classroom Activities

A. Given a teacher-written story, the students will replace the highlighted repetitive noun with a pronoun.

B. Teacher will model a writing piece that has no adjectives. Students will rewrite the piece using meaningful descriptive adjectives.

C. Students will read a paragraph they have written to a peer. The peer will state one thing he or she liked about the paragraph, ask one question, and give one suggestion to improve the writing.

D. Teacher will model by reading a story with a good beginning and ending, then give the students a story with a weak beginning and ending. Students will revise the beginning and ending to make them more exciting and engaging.

Differentiated Instruction

→ Given a teacher-written story, the students will replace the highlighted respective word by circling one of two words that best completes the sentence and avoids repetition.

→ Given a writing piece with no adjectives, students will work together as a class to rewrite the piece, using good descriptive adjectives from a list of "great words."

→ Given a "boring" paragraph, students will read the paragraph aloud and state at least three ways they might improve the paragraph.

→ Presented with a story and three beginnings and endings for it, students will select the beginning and ending that are most interesting and descriptive.

Integration of Real-Life Topics

- **Career Awareness/Work Related**
  Given a previously composed job advertisement for the school newspaper, students will share the ad and discuss layout and wording choices to make it a more eye-catching ad.

- **Home and Family**
  Given a friendly letter that is lengthy and wordy, students will combine short sentences for clarity and remove sentences irrelevant to the central idea.

- **Leisure Time**
  After writing a fictional story to read to a class of younger children, students will underline each verb, check that they are the most precise verbs, and add at least four adverbs.

- **Community Living**
  Using a previously completed letter to a local community business or government office, each student will read aloud his or her letter to a peer. Students will revise any phrases that are difficult to read aloud or are difficult to follow.

- **Emotional/Physical Health**
  After writing a class paragraph focusing on a healthy lifestyle, students will revise word choice and sentence length so the paragraph can be read by students at a lower grade level.

Notes

_____

_____

_____

_____

_____

_____

_____

_____

_____

_____

_____

_____

_____

_____

WRITING / Postwriting

Editing and Revising Content

Classroom Activities

A. Students will be given three paragraphs written by the teacher and will rank the content of each as "Unsatisfactory," "Satisfactory," or "Above Average" according to a rubric of specific evaluation criteria. They will complete a brief written evaluation defending their choices.

B. Students will focus on a recently developed personal sample of their writing (one to two paragraphs) and will self-evaluate their word choices. They will develop a written critique about two specific strengths and two weaknesses in their word choices.

C. Given sample written products by the teacher, students will apply an evaluation checklist to assess the degree to which the author uses voice. They will list specific areas where the use of the author's voice is weak.

D. Students will revise their own written paragraph draft and develop a final product with a focus on the following points: (a) the main idea/topic is followed by an appropriate introduction and conclusion, (b) relevant information is provided by sentences that vary in forms of type, length, and use of figurative words, and (c) the piece holds audience interest.

Differentiated Instruction

→ Students will be given three paragraphs written by the teacher. Small groups of students will review evaluation criteria and apply them to an evaluation of the three writing samples. A joint written evaluation will be developed and shared with the class.

→ Using a recently developed personal writing sample, pairs of students will assist each other in the evaluation and critique of word choices. They will create an outline identifying two strengths and two weaknesses in word choice.

→ Groups of students will collaborate on the process of evaluating the use of author's voice in a specific written product. They will discuss and list areas where the use of the author's voice is weak.

→ Students will revise their own written paragraph after highlighting with different colors the sentences that exemplify each revision point: (a) the main idea/topic is followed by an appropriate introduction and conclusion, (b) relevant information is provided by sentences that vary in forms of type, length, and use of figurative words, and (c) the piece holds audience interest.

Integration of Real-Life Topics

- **Career Awareness/Work Related**
As part of a peer tutoring service-learning project, students will assist students in other classes with the evaluation of their writing assignments, including suggested revisions.
- **Home and Family**
After using a recipe that concluded with an "unsatisfactory" food product, students will revise the recipe with the goal of a tastier outcome.
- **Leisure Time**
Students will revise the dialogue of a school play so that a younger group of students can more easily perform it.
- **Community Living**
Given an upcoming deadline, students will revise a proposed article for the school newspaper to reflect better organization.
- **Emotional/Physical Health**
Students will assist an elderly relative (e.g., grandparent) or neighbor by revising and/or rewriting

their personal correspondence (letters/notes), helping with vocabulary and word choice as needed.

Notes

_____

_____

_____

_____

_____

_____

_____

_____

WRITING / Postwriting

Editing and Revising Content

Classroom Activities

A. Given examples of narrative reports and/or expository or persuasive writing, students will create an evaluation list showing strengths, weaknesses, and suggestions for revisions.

B. Provided with a copy of a selected piece of published writing, students will highlight in one color the areas that they would keep without revising and highlight in another color the areas that they feel need revision.

C. After writing an article for the school newspaper, small groups of students will use a set of teacher-provided criteria to discuss specific strengths and weaknesses, focusing on facts, arguments, opinions, support, and overall clarity.

D. Using a previously written narrative, students will revise their product by providing additional dialogue and enhancing word choice.

Differentiated Instruction

→ Given examples of narrative reports and/or expository or persuasive writing, and a teacher-made evaluation form, small groups of students will complete the form to identify strengths and weaknesses. They will discuss suggestions for revision of one piece of writing.

→ Provided with a copy of a paragraph chosen by the teacher for the individual child, children will highlight in one color areas they would keep without revising and highlight in another color areas they feel need revision.

→ Small groups of students will discuss a school newspaper article. They will offer evaluative suggestions and collectively dictate to the teacher or classroom aide a list of possible revisions.

→ Using a previously written narrative, pairs of students will suggest revisions, focusing on details of events and strong, descriptive adjectives.

Integration of Real-Life Topics

- **Career Awareness/Work Related**
  Given a description of a specific job and its responsibilities, students will revise the job description to make it more to their personal liking.

- **Home and Family**
  Provided with an initial draft of a letter to their parents that attempts to persuade the parents to grant an additional home privilege, students will evaluate their letters, ensuring that they contain enough persuasive details.

- **Leisure Time**
  Given an article of a popular sports event (e.g., game, match), students will revise the article to reflect a completely different outcome.

- **Community Living**
  Given a letter to the editor in a local publication, students will evaluate the presented argument by making a list of counterpoints.

- **Emotional/Physical Health**
  Pairs of students will jointly write a description of a recent bullying situation and then revise the participants' actions and reactions to create a more positive outcome.

Notes

_____

WRITING / Postwriting

Editing Mechanics

Classroom Activities

A. Given a short sentence written without any spacing between words, the class will listen to the sentence and together determine where spaces should be placed.

B. After having drawn a family picture and labeling each family member, children will check each person's name to be sure it begins with a capital letter and has lowercase letters for the rest.

C. When listening to prewritten simple sentences, children will signal a "thumbs down" when they hear a sentence with improper subject–verb agreement (e.g., "He have no pets").

D. Given a previously written Language Experience chart, children will take turns circling each capital letter and period and will tell why each is used.

Differentiated Instruction

→ Given a sentence strip containing a short sentence without any spacing between words, children will cut apart the sentence into individual words and move the words to show proper spacing.

→ After having drawn a family picture, children will dictate each person's name and will discuss which letters should be capitalized.

→ Given several pairs of prewritten sentences, small groups of children will discuss and decide which of each pair shows proper subject–verb agreement (e.g., "She has two pets").

→ Given a previously written Language Experience chart, children will together find each capital letter, trace it, and discuss why it is capitalized.

Integration of Real-Life Topics

• **Career Awareness/Work Related**
After drawing a picture of a favorite career and labeling the career, children will check their spelling on a class-made list of careers.

• **Home and Family**
After helping to write the family's chore chart for the week, children will find each person's name to be sure that it is capitalized.

• **Leisure Time**
Given a dictated letter to Santa, children will place a small mark in yellow after each word to highlight proper spacing.

• **Community Living**
After writing a group thank-you letter for a visit to a local merchant, students will reread the letter and clap when they detect a punctuation mark.

• **Emotional/Physical Health**
Children will write an "I Feel . . ." book illustrating each chosen emotion. They will then reread their book and decide which emotions warrant an exclamation point instead of a period.

Notes

_____

_____

_____

_____

_____

_____

_____

_____

_____

_____

_____

Editing Mechanics

Classroom Activities

A. Students will choose a piece of writing from their writing folders, circle each sight word, and check the spelling on the classroom word wall.

B. In a small group, children will read their writing for the group to "edit by ear" and make suggestions to each other to improve subject–verb agreement and tenses.

C. Pairs of students will intentionally write a short story without any punctuation. They will then switch with another pair of students and add proper punctuation.

D. Given a simple editor's checklist, students will independently check their own work for capitalization, punctuation, spelling, and so forth, by marking each usage with a crayon.

Differentiated Instruction

→ Given a teacher-written piece of writing with several spelling errors on chart paper, students will circle a sight word and check its spelling on the classroom word wall. If incorrect, they will correct the spelling on the chart paper.

→ The teacher will read a piece of writing to small groups of students. Each student will state or suggest how the writing can be improved in regard to subject–verb agreement and tenses.

→ The teacher will present a short written paragraph with errors in punctuation. A pair of students will circle the errors in punctuation, and another pair of students will correct the punctuation.

→ Given a simple editor's checklist displayed on the board, students will take turns checking the piece of writing displayed on an overhead for errors in capitalization, punctuation, and spelling.

Integration of Real-Life Topics

• **Career Awareness/Work Related**
After preparing a set of questions for a career-focused interview of a parent, students will check each other's questions to be sure each ends with a question mark.

• **Home and Family**
When writing gift tags in the process of wrapping holiday presents, children will review each one to be sure that all names are properly capitalized.

• **Leisure Time**
Given their own personal diary from the previous year, children will choose one entry and use newly learned spelling and punctuation skills to rewrite it.

• **Community Living**
Prior to a neighborhood kickball game, children will make posters that advertise the event. Each poster will be checked by a partner to verify proper spelling.

• **Emotional/Physical Health**
After writing detailed New Year's resolutions, students will exchange papers and reread them to check that everything is written in the future tense. They will circle any verbs to be changed.

Notes

Editing Mechanics

Classroom Activities

A. Given a sample of a student writing piece (from a previous class) that is typed onto an overhead, the class will discuss and edit the piece for mechanics and conventions.

B. With a partner, children will use an orange pen to note mechanical errors in their own writing and then trade and use a blue pen to mark errors on their partner's paper.

C. After looking up X number of words on the word wall, students will type their writing on the computer and use the spelling and grammar checks.

D. On a daily basis, the teacher will write a grammatically incorrect sentence on the board. Following their own daily journal entry, students will write the corrected sentence in their journals.

Differentiated Instruction

→ Given a copy of a writing piece and the same writing piece displayed on an overhead, the class will discuss and edit the piece with the teacher and make the necessary corrections on the handout while the teacher makes the stated corrections on the overhead.

→ When shown a piece of writing on chart paper, one student will point to a mechanical error. A second student will state what the error is. In each case, the rest of the class will give a "thumbs up" if correct or a "thumbs down" if incorrect and will then correct it.

→ After looking up X number of words on the word wall, students will dictate their writing to a fifth-grade friend who will type it into the computer. They will together complete spelling and grammatical checks.

→ On a daily basis, the teacher will write a grammatically incorrect sentence on the board. Students will take turns coming up to the board to make a correction.

Integration of Real-Life Topics

• **Career Awareness/Work Related**
Given a previously written description of a person's career, students will review the description with a focus on combining simple sentences into compound sentences where appropriate.

• **Home and Family**
Siblings will each write a wish list from a current toy catalog. They will then exchange lists and use the catalog to check the facts (price, page, and spelling).

• **Leisure Time**
After writing a short skit to perform with friends at a sleep-over, students will review the punctuation to be sure that it will signal appropriate expression when spoken.

• **Community Living**
Before painting pencil-sketched neighborhood garage sale signs, students will review the mechanics, spacing, and type size to ensure an eye-catching presentation.

• **Emotional/Physical Health**
After writing a letter of apology to an adult, students will ask a friend to point out spelling errors and punctuation errors.

Notes

_____

_____

_____

_____

_____

_____

_____

_____

_____

_____

WRITING / Postwriting

Editing Mechanics

Classroom Activities

A. Using a finished piece from their writing folders, students will read the piece backward, word-by-word, to focus on spelling and mechanics (without a focus on meaning).

B. Given a familiar picture book, students will undertake a punctuation search to find and list the forms of punctuation the author used.

C. Using a website such as harcourtschool.com, students will practice proofreading in several game formats.

D. Following a teacher-made rubric for editing, students will score their own writing and later make changes to improve their score.

Differentiated Instruction

→ Using a finished piece of writing that has been written on sentence strips, groups of three students will take turns reading aloud one sentence backward. The group will then locate any spelling or mechanical errors.

→ Given a familiar picture book page read by the teacher, the students will color a bar graph to show the punctuation present on their page.

→ Using a game format from a website such as harcourtschool.com, students will demonstrate for a "Kinderpal" how to check each sentence for proper punctuation.

→ Following a teacher-made rubric for editing, the students will form small groups and take turns asking each writer a rubric-based question (e.g., "Do you have all of the names capitalized?").

Integration of Real-Life Topics

• **Career Awareness/Work Related**
After having written a career classified ad, students will highlight words that need to be spell checked.

• **Home and Family**
When helping a younger sibling or friend write a letter to a relative, children will review the letter and check the handwriting for legibility.

• **Leisure Time**
Using a recent text message from a friend, children will rewrite the message following standard spelling and grammar conventions.

• **Community Living**
Upon reading a newsletter from a local municipal department, students will review a column from the letter, highlighting any words they would like to check in the dictionary.

• **Emotional/Physical Health**
After brainstorming about a list of symptoms of the common cold, each child will search for two of the words on the Internet to check their spelling and grammatical usage.

Notes

_____

_____

_____

_____

_____

_____

_____

_____

_____

_____

_____

_____

WRITING / Postwriting

Editing Mechanics

Classroom Activities

A. Given two sample compositions already evaluated by the teacher—one as "Excellent" and one as "Unsatisfactory"—students will proofread each sample and identify specific strengths and errors, focusing on capitalization, punctuation, word usage, and grammar.

B. Given a sample of a standardized English/language arts test paragraph, students will practice editing by locating and highlighting all mechanical errors. The errors will be corrected together as a class.

C. Given a page from a current content-area text that the teacher has altered to present a variety of mechanical errors, students will analyze and edit the text.

D. Students will select one of their own previous writing pieces for proofreading and editing. They will correct any errors so that the final product can be "published" in a class booklet to be shared at a school open house.

Differentiated Instruction

→ Provided with a teacher-made evaluation checklist poster and copies of an "Excellent" writing sample and an "Unsatisfactory" writing sample, students will discuss the strengths and weaknesses related to capitalization and punctuation.

→ Given an online sample of a standardized English/language arts test paragraph, students will locate and correct "high priority" skill errors as indicated by specific state standards or student IEPs.

→ Given a sample paragraph from a current content-area text that the teacher has altered to present a variety of mechanical errors and has put on an overhead, students will discuss and correct the errors.

→ Provided with access to assistive technology (AT) and support from an AT specialist, students will edit and prepare a piece of writing to be published in a class booklet to be shared at a school open house.

Integration of Real-Life Topics

• **Career Awareness/Work Related**
After developing a first draft of a report on a future career choice, students will proofread and edit for basic capitalization and punctuation.

• **Home and Family**
Students will assist a younger sibling or friend in addressing an envelope in the proper format so that it can be mailed.

• **Leisure Time**
Students will review and edit a copy of an application for a youth sports league or summer camp. With parental assistance, they will check their facts as well as mechanical skills.

• **Community Living**
Students will edit a brief letter of inquiry to the local YMCA or other civic organization. Their focus will be on mechanics, vocabulary, and overall organization.

• **Emotional/Physical Health**
With a focus on emotionally sensitive dialogue, students will review a story depicting a social issue (e.g., bullying, cliques) and will edit the story's dialogue for correct comma and quotation mark usage.

Notes

_____

_____

_____

_____

_____

_____

_____

_____

_____

_____

_____

WRITING / Postwriting

GRADE 5

Editing Mechanics

<table>
<tr><td colspan="2"></td></tr>
</table>

Classroom Activities

A. Provided with three anonymous writing samples that the teacher has evaluated, but not disclosed, as "Excellent," "Adequate," and "Unsatisfactory," students will use a copy-editing checklist to identify and highlight specific mechanical errors in each sample.

B. Students will assign an overall grade of "Excellent," "Adequate," or "Unsatisfactory" to each of three writing samples. The class will share their evaluations, compare them to the teacher's evaluations, and then do necessary corrections to make all three "Excellent."

C. Students will focus on self-editing of a recent personal writing piece by employing an editing guide, such as *REVISE* (Issacson, 2004) or *TOWER* (Hoover & Patton, 2006), or an error monitoring strategy, such as "C.O.P.S." (Mercer & Mercer, 2001).

D. Given a set of cards containing famous quotes without any punctuation, students will add the proper punctuation for the quotations.

Differentiated Instruction

→ The teacher will provide students with a writing sample with a small number of errors. Students will use a copy-editing checklist to identify and highlight specific mechanical errors.

→ On a SMART Board or overhead, the teacher will show students two writing pieces that each have strengths and weaknesses highlighted. The group will discuss the specific skill examples necessary to have a rating of "Excellent" and make any needed modifications for each sample.

→ Working in pairs, students will assist each other with the editing of a recent personal writing piece. Each student will use a different editing guide or error monitoring strategy, such as *REVISE, TOWER,* or C.O.P.S., to assist their partner.

→ Given a set of cards containing famous quotes, some of which are missing some punctuation, students will find the quotes that need editing and will decide collectively the appropriate correction(s).

Integration of Real-Life Topics

• **Career Awareness/Work Related**
As part of a group reviewing the dialogue for a class play, students will analyze the script, identify errors, and make appropriate corrections.

• **Home and Family**
Students will assist parents in editing and revising an advertisement for a local Penny Saver or Community Shopper or for publication on eBay or another Internet auction site.

• **Leisure Time**
As part of a classroom incentive, when instant messaging with a friend, students will challenge themselves to avoid "computer-speak," using standard English instead.

• **Community Living**
When preparing for a class or group fund-raiser, students will access previous years' advertisements and will edit them to reflect current information.

• **Emotional/Physical Health**
Given a personal note written in a state of anger, frustration, or other strong emotion, students will revisit the note after having calmed down and edit it for grammar, spelling, and especially word choices.

Notes

_____

WRITING / Postwriting

Listening

Speaking

Introduction

Researchers have suggested that the area of oral language (listening, speaking) is a foundation skill for early elementary learning and a key predictor of student success in reading, writing, and overall literacy at later grade levels (Education Update, 1999). In addition, many students with disabilities, particularly learning disabilities, often exhibit significant problems in the area of oral language skills, including oral reading (Polloway et al., 2004).

Although many forms of human communication, such as technology, art, music, and kinesthetics, are employed in everyday life (including elementary classrooms), oral language is the major medium used to communicate thoughts, feelings, ideas, emotions, directions, and beliefs (Hammill & Newcomer, 2008; Newcomer & Hammill, 2008; Nippold, 2007). The daily use of oral language is essential not only in school classrooms but throughout everyday life situations and relationships, such as home and family, careers, community, and personal relationships (Polloway, Patton, & Serna, 2008). This section on oral language is centered on the development of student listening and speaking skills. Each outline will provide teachers with suggestions for a variety of group and class activities, differentiation of these activities for students with disabilities, and a number of suggestions for how teachers can integrate real-life skills activities with listening and speaking skills.

Listening

Classroom Activities

A. In a small group, one child (or the teacher) will begin a story by saying the first sentence aloud. The next person will listen to the first sentence, then contribute the next sentence, and so on.

B. Children will listen as the teacher drops marbles, one by one, into an empty coffee can. The children will silently count how many went in and write the number on a white board.

C. Given different picture cards of farm animals, each child will try to find other children with the same animal. With eyes closed, they will slowly walk and make the sound of the animal (e.g., *baa* for a sheep). They will listen to try to find other children who are making the same sound so they can form a group.

D. Provided with groups of objects from the same category (e.g., four different balls, leaves, or desserts), the children will listen carefully as the teacher describes one of the items; the children will then identify the chosen item.

Differentiated Instruction

→ Working with small groups, the teacher will begin a familiar story by saying the first sentence aloud. He or she will show visual prompts to a student, who will continue the story with the next sentence, and so on.

→ Children will listen and follow along on a number line as the teacher drops marbles, one by one, into an empty coffee can. The children will state the number.

→ Given different picture cards of farm animals, pairs of children will try to find other pairs with the same animal. They will walk arm-in-arm, making the sound of their animal (e.g., *moo* for a cow). They will listen to try to find the other pairs who are making the same sound.

→ Provided with two different objects from the same category (e.g., two balls, two leaves, two desserts), children will listen carefully as the teacher describes one of the items. The children will collaboratively decide which item is being described.

Integration of Real-Life Topics

- **Career Awareness/Work Related**
  Children will listen to a brief description of a familiar career. They will identify the career by finding its corresponding picture.

- **Home and Family**
  Using a sample recipe, a parent or sibling will read each step to the child. The child will follow the directions to measure, mix, pour, and so forth.

- **Leisure Time**
  Children will play the card game Go Fish. They will listen to their opponent's request for a particular card while playing the game.

- **Community Living**
  While going on a neighborhood walk, children will listen to the sounds of the neighborhood to later contribute to a class chart or book.

- **Emotional/Physical Health**
  Children will listen while playing the familiar game Simon Says. The commands will focus on elements of physical fitness.

Notes

_____

_____

_____

_____

_____

_____

_____

_____

_____

_____

ORAL LANGUAGE / Listening

Listening

Classroom Activities	Differentiated Instruction
A. In a class circle, each child will complete a sentence such as, "My favorite fruit is _____" or "Today's weather makes me feel _____" or "The best thing I did over the weekend was _____." After four or five children have had their turn, the group will stop to see who remembers the sentences of the children who just said them. They will then continue with the next four or five children, and so on.	→ In a small-group circle, each child will complete a sentence such as, "My favorite fruit is _____" or "Today's weather makes me feel _____." After each child completes the sentence, the group will collaboratively paraphrase or restate the sentence.
B. Working with partners or in groups of three, children will share an opinion such as, "The best color is _____" or "I really like to eat _____ for lunch." After they share, each child will tell the class the answer of their partner or someone else in their group.	→ Working with partners or in groups of three, children will share an opinion such as, "The best color is _____" or "I really like to eat _____ for lunch." The partner of one of the other children will choose from pictures the one that represents the stated opinion. They will then share those opinions with the class.
C. Children will listen as the teacher (or other children) states items that belong to a particular category. Listeners will try to identify the category.	→ Children will listen as the teacher states items that belong to a particular category. Listeners will identify the category by pointing to the word card that states its title.
D. Children will sit in a circle with their eyes closed. The teacher will tap one child to read a phrase or sentence. The class will guess the identity of the speaker.	→ Children will sit in a circle with their eyes closed. The teacher will tap one child to state a phrase or sentence. The class will guess the identity of the speaker.

Integration of Real-Life Topics

- **Career Awareness/Work Related**
  Children will listen to directions of two or three steps for completing a classroom job.

- **Home and Family**
  Children will ask a family member to tell them some ideas of items they would like to receive for a holiday gift.

- **Leisure Time**
  Children will listen to a symphony version of Peter and the Wolf. They will collectively discuss and identify characters and instruments.

- **Community Living**
  On a trip to the local farm market, children will listen to various merchants to find out which fruits and/or vegetables are in season.

- **Emotional/Physical Health**
  Children will play Healthy Choices Bingo and listen to clues that identify a healthy lifestyle choice or activity on the Bingo cards.

Notes

_____

_____

_____

_____

_____

_____

_____

_____

_____

_____

ORAL LANGUAGE / Listening

Listening

Classroom Activities

A. With the goal of making a class "All About Us" book, each child will bring in several objects that illustrate things the child likes. After explaining each item, the class will help in writing a list of things the child likes (without seeing the objects).

B. Students will listen to a story with distinctive characters (e.g., Shrek, SpongeBob Squarepants). They will then retell the story with puppets for the rest of the class.

C. The teacher will read or recite a story in which one word per sentence will be separated into phonemes (e.g., /k/ /a/ /t/). As the teacher reads the segmented word, the children will listen and blend the word so the story can continue.

D. Teacher and children will sing "Willaby (or Willoughby) Wallaby Woo" together. As each verse approaches, children will attentively listen to figure out whose name will be identified. They will point to the child whose name they anticipate hearing (before the name is sung).

Differentiated Instruction

→ With the goal of making a group "Fruits We Like" or "Our Favorite Sports" book, each child will state his or her chosen topic. The other children will take turns making an entry in the book, with one entry for each child.

→ Students will listen to a story with two distinctive characters (e.g., Shrek and SpongeBob Squarepants). In pairs, they will discuss the characters and make a series of character attributes (e.g., *persistent, brave, careless*) word cards to share with the class.

→ As the teacher reads or recites a short story, he or she will frequently stop briefly for the students to reiterate a main point and provide phonemic awareness practice (e.g., the teacher reads, "Cinderella lost her /sh/ /oo/." The teacher then asks, "What did she lose?" Children respond, "Her shoe!").

→ Teacher and children will sing "Willaby (or Willoughby) Wallaby Woo" together. As each verse is sung, children will point to the child whose name is identified.

Integration of Real-Life Topics

- **Career Awareness/Work Related**
  Children will listen to a book on tape that details job responsibilities of a career of interest.

- **Home and Family**
  Children will listen to a parent describe two or three possible family events. The children will later vote for their preferred activity.

- **Leisure Time**
  After listening to the items to pack for a sleep-over, children will pack a bag with all of the items.

- **Community Living**
  Children will listen to a high school student identify items that can and cannot be recycled. They will then sort their own refuse.

- **Emotional/Physical Health**
  Children will play a game of Exercise Simon Says (which would include exercise-related directions).

Notes

_____

_____

_____

_____

_____

_____

_____

_____

_____

ORAL LANGUAGE / Listening

Listening

Classroom Activities

A. In small groups, each child will describe something good in a negative way (e.g., ice cream cone—"It is too cold and creamy. It's too pointy on the bottom. It's too sweet, and it's very messy.") Other children will try to determine what was described.

B. The teacher will read aloud a short magazine or newspaper article. The class will then devise a good headline or title for the article.

C. Each child will have a picture of a famous person (real or fictional) taped on his or her back. Each child's partner will tell about the person, including descriptions and facts, until the first child can determine who is being described.

D. When presented with a "What would you do if . . . ?" scenario, partners will discuss possible responses, decide on one appropriate response, and illustrate their idea.

Differentiated Instruction

→ In small groups, each child will describe in detail a familiar item. The other children will listen and try to figure out what was described.

→ The teacher will read aloud a short magazine or newspaper article. The children will then create a small poster using a program such as Microsoft Word. They will find clip art to illustrate the main idea(s) of the article.

→ Each child will have a picture of a famous person (real or fictional) taped on his or her back. Each child's partner, using a list of key points/clues, will tell about the person until the first child can determine who is being described.

→ When presented with a "What would you do if . . . ?" scenario, small groups of children will discuss responses suggested by the teacher and decide on one appropriate response.

Integration of Real-Life Topics

• **Career Awareness/Work Related**
While watching a video about careers/jobs in other cultures, children will listen for similarities and differences to include in a later discussion.

• **Home and Family**
Children will listen to local weather reports on three different radio stations. They will then help the family with outdoor recreation plans.

• **Leisure Time**
Children will listen to a book on tape during a car trip or airplane ride.

• **Community Living**
As part of a neighborhood watch system, children will listen to news and/or police scanner reports during a crisis. They will help disseminate the information to neighbors.

• **Emotional/Physical Health**
Children will listen to a walking or walking/running CD to direct their daily exercise routine.

Notes

Listening

Classroom Activities

A. After listening to one of a variety of listening situations (e.g., story read aloud, song lyrics, reading of a poem or play script), children will identify and discuss details, vocabulary, facts, generalizations, and so forth, from their listening.

B. While listening to a classroom read-aloud, children will visualize events in the story. They will then share and compare their visualizations with those of a partner before they summarize the story in writing.

C. After selecting a favorite period of history, students will find a story, poem, or play that is set in that period. They will listen to the story, poem, or play; summarize the major events/themes; and illustrate the connection to the time period.

D. Students will listen to a story read aloud by the teacher. They will take notes as they read to assist them in responding to a variety of questions about the story.

Differentiated Instruction

→ While listening to one of a variety of listening situations (e.g., story read aloud, song lyrics, reading of a poem or play script), children will identify and discuss one category of information (e.g., details OR vocabulary OR facts).

→ While listening to a classroom read-aloud and discussing the story with a partner, students will refer to visual clues (e.g., illustrations, photographs) to help them retell the story.

→ Following a media-rich (e.g., stories, poems, plays, video) unit on a period of time in history, pairs of students will assist each other in illustrating the facts they have heard.

→ Students will listen to a story read aloud by the teacher. They will complete a graphic organizer to guide their note-taking for the purpose of responding to a variety of questions about the story.

Integration of Real-Life Topics

- **Career Awareness/Work Related**
  Students will listen to classmates read a persuasive essay designed to "promote" a specific career. They will then share their own opinions of the career.

- **Home and Family**
  In preparation for a family trip, students will listen to recordings describing tourist attractions. They will then list the attractions they would like to visit.

- **Leisure Time**
  Students will listen to lyrics of songs focusing on a (teacher-approved) area of interest. They will later interpret the lyrics for classmates.

- **Community Living**
  Students will listen to a local radio advertisement. They will record pertinent information for someone else's use.

- **Emotional/Physical Health**
  After listening to a variety of prerecorded voice-mail messages, students will evaluate and/or categorize each according to pre-set criteria (e.g., socially appropriate, appropriate only for peers, complete/incomplete content).

Notes

_____

_____

_____

_____

_____

_____

_____

_____

_____

_____

_____

Listening

Classroom Activities

A. Working in pairs, students will read to each other textbook selections that are rich with figurative language. With a dictionary or thesaurus available, they will classify words and phrases as idioms, clichés, slang words, and so forth.

B. Students will listen to spoken material (recorded for multiple usage). After listening to it several times, they will respond to a variety of discussion and/or writing prompts.

C. Provided with a variety of poorly written essay selections, students will listen to them and identify specific points that are incomplete, redundant, trivial, irrelevant, and so forth.

D. Students will choose a popular radio advertisement. They will listen to identify various aspects of it (e.g., speaker's purpose, intended audience, persuasive language, bias).

Differentiated Instruction

→ Students will listen to the teacher read a textbook passage rich with figurative language. They will then discuss and classify various phrases and types of figurative language.

→ Students will repeatedly listen to recorded spoken material while following a written outline of that material. They will then respond to a variety of discussion and/or writing prompts.

→ A small cooperative group will listen to a poorly written essay. They will fill in an outline, providing an example for each heading (e.g., "Redundancies," "Trivial Statements," "Incomplete Information").

→ Students will choose a popular radio advertisement. They will create an outline (in words and/or illustrations) of the main components of the ad (e.g., central theme, purpose of the ad).

Integration of Real-Life Topics

• **Career Awareness/Work Related**
Children will listen to various workers speak about "A Day in the Life of a _____." Children will take notes about the various responsibilities of each career.

• **Home and Family**
Students will watch a Food Channel program illustrating a specific recipe. They will take notes on the directions for preparing the recipe at home.

• **Leisure Time**
When preparing for an upcoming class play, students will listen to one another "read" for the various parts. They will collectively decide who should play which part.

• **Community Living**
Students will listen to an explanation of the voter registration process and voting procedures. They will then register for and vote in a mock election.

• **Emotional/Physical Health**
Students will listen to a health professional explain specific precautions to prevent the spread of colds and flu. They will then share the information with their family.

Notes

_____

_____

_____

_____

_____

_____

_____

_____

_____

_____

_____

_____

_____

Speaking

Classroom Activities

A. Once a week, children will participate in "Show and Tell." They will tell two or three facts and answer one or two questions from classmates regarding the item they brought to school.

B. Children will contribute an idea for a setting, character, event, phrase, or other item while writing a class experience story.

C. Using a set of three or four related pictures, children will tell the story represented by the pictures.

D. Children will dictate a recipe for a make-believe dish. They will include ingredients and procedures.

Differentiated Instruction

→ Once a week, children will participate in "Show and Tell." They will tell the class at least one fact regarding the item they brought to school.

→ During the writing of a class experience story, children will contribute an idea for a setting, character, event, or phrase when asked a specific question (e.g., "What will the character say next?").

→ Using a self-drawn picture, children will tell the class what is represented by the picture.

→ Children will dictate an ingredient list for a make-believe dish/recipe.

Integration of Real-Life Topics

• **Career Awareness/Work Related**
When shown a picture of a person at work, the students will state the career and describe what the person is doing in the picture.

• **Home and Family**
Students will draw a picture of their family and, using this picture, describe to the class the members of their family.

• **Leisure Time**
Students will dictate to the teacher information about their favorite leisure-time activity to be included on an "All About Me" bulletin board.

• **Community Living**
After taking a walk in the community, students will describe to the class their favorite part of the walk.

• **Emotional/Physical Health**
After a visit by a dental hygienist, the students will explain one reason why it is important to take care of our teeth.

Notes

_____

_____

_____

_____

_____

_____

_____

_____

_____

_____

_____

ORAL LANGUAGE / Speaking

Speaking

Classroom Activities

A. Following a nature walk, children will describe with as much detail as possible an item they saw.

B. During a handwriting lesson, children will give the teacher very precise and specific directions to form a letter (e.g., "Make a straight line down from the middle line to the bottom line").

C. After hearing and discussing a story (with a clear plot and conclusion), children will use puppets to reenact the story, including sequenced events and dialogue.

D. As part of a morning circle time, children will orally respond to a prompt such as, "The best part of my vacation was . . ." or "Today I will make sure that I . . . ."

Differentiated Instruction

→ Following a nature walk, children will state an adjective to describe an item seen on the walk.

→ During a handwriting lesson, children will use cue cards (e.g., diagonal, straight line, small circle, start at dotted line) to help give the teacher precise directions to form a letter.

→ After hearing and discussing a story (with a clear plot and conclusion), children will use one puppet to reenact one character's part in the story.

→ As part of a morning circle time, the children will orally respond to a direct question asked by the teacher (e.g., "What did you do for fun over the weekend?").

Integration of Real-Life Topics

• **Career Awareness/Work Related**
In their own words, students will describe to an older friend at least one responsibility of a firefighter.

• **Home and Family**
Students will describe to their parents the necessary steps to follow in an Exit Drills in the Home (E.D.I.T.H.) drill.

• **Leisure Time**
Students will tell a classmate about their favorite winter activity (e.g., sledding), explaining how to perform the activity.

• **Community Living**
Students will draw a picture of at least one way they can help their community. The students will then describe to the class what they are doing in the picture.

• **Emotional/Physical Health**
From a picture list of healthy and unhealthy food choices, the students will pick out a healthy food and explain why the food is healthy.

Notes

_____

ORAL LANGUAGE / Speaking

Speaking

Classroom Activities

A. Children will memorize and recite a seasonal or motivational poem, chant, or rap for their classmates.

B. After reading or listening to the first section of a storybook, students will make illogical, unreasonable, and unlikely predictions about the story's outcome.

C. Children will contribute to a class brainstorming session at the beginning of a new unit. They will each share several thoughts, facts, or other statements pertaining to the new unit.

D. Children will retell a familiar story, making changes to the setting, characters, and outcome.

Differentiated Instruction

→ Children will memorize and recite one line from a seasonal or motivational poem, chant, or rap for their classmates.

→ After reading or listening to the first section of a storybook, students will make a logical prediction about the story's outcome.

→ Children will contribute to a small-group brainstorming session at the beginning of a new unit. They will each share one thought, fact, or other statement pertaining to the new unit.

→ Children will retell a familiar story, making changes to the setting, characters, or outcome.

Integration of Real-Life Topics

- **Career Awareness/Work Related**
  Children will interview a school worker to find out details about his or her job.

- **Home and Family**
  For an upcoming birthday party, children will practice introducing their friends to their parents and siblings.

- **Leisure Time**
  Children will demonstrate and explain the equipment for and procedures of fishing.

- **Community Living**
  When selling a product for a community or school fund-raiser, children will explain to customers the purpose of the sale.

- **Emotional/Physical Health**
  During a discussion of scenarios about bullying, students will relate their personal emotions about the situation.

Notes

_____

_____

_____

_____

_____

_____

_____

_____

_____

Speaking

Classroom Activities

A. After researching an unfamiliar subject (e.g., a culture, an unusual animal), children will give an oral report to the class and videotape their oral report.

B. Children will read and recite the daily school news and announcements on the school public address system.

C. In a small group, and using a chosen short story or novel, children will share their opinions of the story by responding to group-generated questions.

D. After reading one chapter of a book, small groups will present a summary to the rest of the class. This summary could be in the form of a skit, a song, narrated pictures, or a simple verbal summary. When all groups are done, the whole book will have been summarized.

Differentiated Instruction

→ After researching a familiar subject, children will give an oral report to the class and/or videotape their oral report.

→ Children will find out the daily temperature and report it to the class and/or on the school public address system.

→ After listening to a story, children will share their opinions of the story by responding to group-generated questions.

→ After reading a selected section of a book (e.g., a page, a paragraph, an event), small groups will present a summary of their section to the rest of the class.

Integration of Real-Life Topics

- **Career Awareness/Work Related**
  With a partner or small group, children will act out, with dialogue, a skit depicting a chosen career.

- **Home and Family**
  With their family, children will brainstorm and discuss pros and cons of a recent vacation, holiday, or other family event.

- **Leisure Time**
  Working with a group of younger children, students will explain the rules of a game to the group.

- **Community Living**
  Following the format prescribed by a 4H group leader, children will research and present a chosen topic at a 4H meeting or county fair.

- **Emotional/Physical Health**
  Children will develop a PowerPoint presentation and script for a talk about healthy habits to be given to a group of peers.

Notes

_____

_____

_____

_____

_____

_____

_____

_____

_____

_____

ORAL LANGUAGE / Speaking

Speaking

Classroom Activities

A. From a variety of photographs depicting speech in everyday life, each student will develop a brief explanation of a photo and then informally tell classmates about the photo.

B. After listening to the lyrics of a teacher-selected song and discussing the message, theme, and/or specific words, students will share their personal views of the lyrics in a small-group discussion.

C. After studying a controversial environmental or political issue, students will develop a brief outline and give a short oral presentation to summarize the issue and present their personal view.

D. Students will interview a classmate who is playing the role of a familiar fictional character. After finding out information of importance and interest, students will present their findings about the character to the class.

Differentiated Instruction

→ From a variety of photographs depicting speech in everyday life and word cards of pertinent vocabulary, each student will develop a brief explanation of a photo and then informally tell classmates about the photo.

→ After listening to a variety of teacher-selected songs, students will choose one song to discuss with a partner. They will then share their personal views of the lyrics in a small-group discussion.

→ Students will read about or watch a media presentation concerning a controversial environmental or political issue. Pairs or groups of three students will discuss the issue and outline a brief summary. Each student will orally share with the class part of the summary as well as his or her personal opinion of the issue.

→ Students will interview a classmate to find out personal information. After finding out pertinent information, students will present their findings about the classmate to the class.

Integration of Real-Life Topics

- **Career Awareness/Work Related**
  Students will choose a career/job of interest and prepare a presentation to explain, describe, and/or demonstrate the job and what they like and do not like about it.

- **Home and Family**
  As part of a family dinner, children and all other family members will tell one thing for which they are thankful and explain why they are thankful.

- **Leisure Time**
  Students will orally present a rationale to convince their parents that they should be allowed to do something (e.g., go to a movie, participate in a sport, have a sleep-over).

- **Community Living**
  As a member of a Girl Scout, Boy Scout, 4H, or FFA group, students will develop a presentation explaining a current project. They will give the presentation to a local service group.

- **Emotional/Physical Health**
  Given a health issue of interest, students will role play how they would deal with that issue or how they would get help for it (e.g., first aid, call 911).

Notes

_____

_____

_____

_____

_____

_____

_____

_____

_____

_____

_____

_____

ORAL LANGUAGE / Speaking

Speaking

Classroom Activities	Differentiated Instruction
A. After researching a famous person from the past, students will organize and present a "Memorial Speech" to the class.	→ After researching a famous person from the past and being given a set of notes in an outline format, students will present a "Memorial Speech" to the class.
B. In pairs, students will research a sports figure. One student will then act as a television or radio reporter. He or she will interview the partner, who will portray the sports figure. The interviewer will ask pertinent questions and follow-up questions. The sports figure will respond as the real person might.	→ In pairs, students will research a sports figure. They will watch several actual interviews and will be provided with a set of generic questions. One student will act as a television or radio reporter and interview the other student, who will portray the sports figure. The interviewer will ask pertinent questions and follow-up questions. The sports figure will respond as the real person might.
C. After watching a political debate, students will reenact the debate, being sure to include relevant facts and issues and/or propaganda.	→ After watching and taking notes from a political debate, students will reenact the debate, following the sequence from their notes.
D. Students will portray "characters" (e.g., judge, lawyers, jury, defendant) in a mock trial. The focus can be any current or historical, factual or fictional issue.	→ Given a prewritten script, students will portray "characters" (e.g., judge, lawyers, jury, defendant) in a mock trial. The script will be used as much or as little as needed during the trial.

Integration of Real-Life Topics

- **Career Awareness/Work Related**
  As part of a Career Day, students will participate in mock job interviews with a professional from their field of choice.

- **Home and Family**
  Children will discuss with family members the rules of the house. The focus should be on constructive discussion, not argument.

- **Leisure Time**
  Children will create a comic strip illustration of an activity they enjoy doing with their family. They will then explain or narrate the illustrations to the class.

- **Community Living**
  As part of a discussion, students will name the various community activities in which their family participates and community services that their family uses.

- **Emotional/Physical Health**
  Students will create and enact a commercial to promote an activity that enhances general health and wellness.

Notes

_____

_____

_____

_____

_____

_____

_____

_____

_____

_____

ORAL LANGUAGE / Speaking

REFERENCES

Archer, A., & Gleason, M. (1989). *Skills for school success.* North Billerica, MA: Curriculum Associates.

Blalock, G., Patton, J. R., Kohler, P., & Bassett, D. (Eds.). (2008). *Transition and students with learning disabilities: Facilitating the movement from school to adult life* (2nd ed.). Austin, TX: Hammill Institute on Disabilities.

Carnine, D. W., Silbert, J., Kame'enui, E. J., & Tarver, S. (2004). *Direct instruction reading* (4th ed.). Upper Saddle River, NJ: Merrill/Prentice Hall.

Cronin, M. E., Patton, J. R., & Wood, S. (2007). *Life skills instruction: A practical guide for integrating real-life content into the curriculum at the elementary and secondary levels for students with special needs or who are placed at risk* (2nd ed.). Austin, TX: PRO-ED.

Crystal, D. (2001). *A dictionary of language* (2nd ed.). Chicago: University of Chicago.

Education Update. (1999, June). *Speaking and listening: The first basic skills.* Alexandria, VA: Association for Supervision and Curriculum.

Goals 2000: Education America Act [America 2000]. (1990). Washington, DC: U.S. Department of Education.

Graham, S., & Harris, K. R. (2005). Improving the writing performance of young struggling writers: Theoretical and programming research from the center on accelerating student learning. *The Journal of Special Education, 39,* 19–33.

Gray, W. S. (1940). Reading and factors influencing reading efficiency. In W. S. Gray (Ed.), *Reading in general education* (pp. 18–44). Washington, DC: American Council on Education.

Hall, T. C. (2002). *NCAC effective classroom practices report: Differentiated instruction* [online]. Retrieved June 2002 from www.cast.org/system/galleries/download/ncac/DifInstrucNov2.pdf

Hammill, D. D. (2004). What we know about correlates of reading. *Exceptional Children, 70*(4), 453–468.

Hammill, D. D., & Bartel, N. R. (Eds.). (2004). *Teaching students with learning and behavioral problems* (7th ed.). Austin, TX: PRO-ED.

Hammill, D. D., & Larsen, S. C. (2009). *Test of written language* (4th ed.). Austin, TX: PRO-ED.

Hammill, D. D., & Newcomer, P L. (2008). *Test of language development–Intermediate* (4th ed.). Austin, TX: PRO-ED.

Hoover, J. J., & Patton, J. R. (2007). *Teaching study skills to students with learning problems: A teacher's guide to meeting diverse needs* (2nd ed.). Austin, TX: PRO-ED.

Hoover, J. J., & Patton, J. R. (2008). The role of special educators in a multilevel instructional system. *Intervention in School and Clinic, 43*(4), 195–202.

Individuals with Disabilities Education Act of 1990, 20 U.S.C. § 1400 *et seq.* (1990) (amended 1997)

Individuals with Disabilities Education Improvement Act of 2004, 20 U.S.C. § 1400 *et seq.* (2004) (reauthorization of IDEA 1990)

Issacson, S. (2004). Instruction that helps students meet state standards in writing. *Exceptionality, 12,* 39–54.

Lipson, M. Y., & Wixson, K. K. (2002). *Assessment and instruction of reading and writing difficulty* (3rd ed.). Boston: Allyn & Bacon.

Mastropieri, M. A., & Scruggs, T. E. (1997). Best practices in promoting reading comprehension in students with learning disabilities. *Remedial and Special Education, 18,* 197–213.

Mather, N., Roberts, R., Hammill, D. P., & Allen, E. (2008). *Test of orthographic competence.* Austin, TX: PRO-ED.

Mercer, C. D., & Mercer, A. R. (2001). *Teaching students with learning problems* (6th ed.). Columbus, OH: Merrill.

Newcomer, P. L., & Hammill, D. D. (2008). *Test of language development–Primary* (4th ed.). Austin, TX: PRO-ED.

Nippold, M. A. (2007). *Later language development* (3rd ed.). Austin, TX: PRO-ED.

No Child Left Behind Act of 2001, 20 U.S.C. 70 § 6301 *et seq.* (2002).

Patton, J. R., Cronin, M. E., & Wood, S. J. (1999). *Infusing real-life topics into existing curricula: Recommended procedures and instructional examples for the elementary, middle, and high school levels.* Austin, TX: PRO-ED.

Polloway, E. A., Miller, L., & Smith, T. E. C. (2004). *Language instruction for students with disabilities* (3rd ed.). Denver, CO: Love.

Polloway, E. A., Patton, J. R., & Serna, L. (2008). *Strategies for teaching learners with special needs* (9th ed.). Upper Saddle River, NJ: Pearson/Merrill/Prentice Hall.

RAND Reading Study Group. (2002). *Reading for understanding: Toward an R and D program in reading comprehension* (Report prepared for the Office of Educational Research and Improvement [OERI]). Arlington, VA: Science and Technology Institute.

Rubin, D. (2000). *Teaching elementary language arts: A balanced approach* (6th ed.). Boston: Allyn & Bacon.

Taylor, R. L. (2009). *Assessment of exceptional students: Educational and psychological procedures* (8th ed.). Upper Saddle River, NJ: Pearson.

Thompson, S., & Thurlow, M. (2001). *State special education outcomes, 2001: A report on state activities at the beginning of a new decade.* Minneapolis: National Center for Educational Outcomes. (ERIC Reproduction No. ED455626)

Troia, G. A. (2005, October). *The writing instructional research we have, the writing instructional research we need.* Paper presented at the first annual Michigan State University Symposium on Literacy Achievement, East Lansing, MI.

Troia, G. A., & Graham, S. (2002). The effectiveness of a highly explicit, teacher directed strategy instruction routine: Changing the writing performance of students with learning disabilities. *Journal of Learning Disabilities, 35,* 290–305.

Wiederholt, J. L., & Bryant, B. R. (2001). *Gray oral reading tests* (4th ed.). Austin, TX: PRO-ED.

Ysseldyke, J., & Olsen, K. (1999). Putting alternate assessments into practice: What to measure and possible sources of data. *Exceptional Children, 65,* 175–185.

INSTRUCTIONAL RESOURCES

I. Language Arts Materials

A. Reading

Dolch Sight Word Games [Computer software]. (1995). Washington, DC: Educational Computer Resources.

Edmark Reading Program (Levels 1, 2). (1992). Austin, TX: PRO-ED.

Invitations to Literacy K–6. (1996). Boston: Houghton Mifflin.

The Lindamood Phoneme Sequencing for Reading Spelling and Speech, Lindamood, P. & Lindamood, P. (2003). Austin, TX: PRO-ED.

Open Court 2002 Series K–6. (2002). New York: Open Court/SRA/McGraw-Hill.

Patterns for Success in Reading and Spelling: A Multisensory Approach to Teaching Phonics and Word Analysis, Henry, M. K. & Redding, N. C. (2002). Austin, TX: PRO-ED.

Phonological Awareness and Primary Phonics, Gunning, T. G. (2000). Boston: Allyn & Bacon.

Phonemic Awareness in Young Children: A Classroom Curriculum, Adams, J., Foorman, B. R., Lundberg, I., & Beeler, T. (1998). Baltimore: Brookes.

Phonological Awareness Training for Reading, Torgeson, J. K. & Bryant, B. R. (1994). Austin, TX: PRO-ED.

Reading Mastery (Distar). (2002). New York: SRA/McGraw-Hill.

Reading Mastery Plus/SRA (1995). DeSoto TX: SRA/McGraw-Hill.

Reading Recovery. (1992). Columbus, OH: Office of Education Research.

Reading Milestones: An Alternative Reading Program (3rd ed.), Quigley, S. P., McAnally, P. L., Rose, S., & King, C. M. (2001). Austin, TX: PRO-ED.

Teaching Children to Read: An Evidence-Based Assessment of the Scientific Research on Reading and Its Implications for Reading Instruction (NIH Publication No. 00-4769), National Reading Panel. (2000). Washington, DC: National Institutes of Health, National Institute of Child Health and Human Development.

Wilson Reading System, Wilson, B. A. (1992). Milbury, MA: Wison Language Training Corp.

B. Written Language

The Apple Tree Curriculum for Developing Written Language, Anderson, M. (1999). Austin, TX: PRO-ED.

Bank Street Writer [Computer software]. (n.d.). New York: Scholastic.

Basic Writing Skills: Capitalization and Punctuation, Gleason, M. & Stults, C. (1983a). Chicago: Science Research Associates.

Basic Writing Skills: Sentence Development, Gleason, M. & Stults, C. (1983b). Chicago: Science Research Associates.

Evaluating and Improving Written Expression: A Practical Guide for Teachers (3rd ed.), Hall, J. K., Grimes, A. E., & Salas, B. (1999). Austin, TX: PRO-ED.

Expressive Writing 1 and 2, Englemann, S. & Silbert, J. (1983). Chicago: Science Research Associates.

Recipe for Writing and Spelling: An Integrated Program (3rd ed.), Bloom, F. & Coates, D. B. (2007). Austin, TX: PRO-ED.

Sentence Combining: A Composing Book, Strong, W. (1983). New York: Random House.

Stetson Spelling Program (2nd ed.), Stetson, E. G. & Stetson, R. (2001). Austin, TX: PRO-ED.

Student Writing Center [Computer software]. (n.d.). Novato, CA: Riverdeep.

Teaching Competence in Written Language (2nd ed.), Phelps-Terasaki, D. & Phelps-Gunn, T. (2000). Austin, TX: PRO-ED.

Write:OutLoud [Computer software]. (n.d.). Volo, IL: Don Johnston.

C. Oral Language

Concept Builders: Pictures and Activities Based on the Boehm Inventory, Weiner, C., Creighton, J. M., & Lyons, T. S. (1995). Austin, TX: PRO-ED.

Describe It: Games to Build Descriptive Language Skills, Thomas-Kensting, C., McCormack, A., & Satin, S. J. (1996). Austin, TX: PRO-ED.

Figurative Language Cards, Kipping, P. & Gemmer, T. (2002). Austin, TX: PRO-ED.

The Idioms Workbook (2nd ed.), Auslin, M. S. (2003). Austin, TX: PRO-ED.

Library of Early Emergent Vocabulary Photographs. (2001). Austin, TX: PRO-ED.

Multicultural Communication Skills in the Classroom, Adler, S. (1993). Boston: Allyn & Bacon.

Pragmatic Activities for Language Intervention: Semantics, Syntax, and Emerging Literacy, Paul, R. (1992). Austin, TX: PRO-ED.

Workbook for Synonyms, Homonyms, and Antonyms, Rea-Rosenberger, S. (1999). Austin, TX: PRO-ED.

D. Web-Based Resources for Language Arts Instruction

Center for Applied Special Technology. (2006). *Research and development in universal design for learning.* Retrieved August 30, 2006, from http://www.cast.org/research/projects/index.html

Columbia Education Center. (n.d.). *Language arts lesson plans for primary, intermediate and high school.* Retrieved from http://www.col-ed.org/cur/lang.html

Education Podcast Network. (2007). Retrieved March 26, 2007, from http://www.epnweb.org/

Educators Reference Desk (http://www.eduref.org/cgi-bin/lessons.cgi/language_arts). Dozens of links to language arts lessons and resources.

Family Education Network. (2003). *Metaphoric unit poems* [online]. Retrieved June 17, 2003, from http://www.teachervision.com/lesson-plans/lesson-5454.html

Illinois State Board of Education. (2003). *English language arts performance descriptors.* Retrieved June 9, 2003, from http://www.isbe.state.il.us/ils/default.htm

LD Online. (2003a). Retrieved June 13, 2003, from http://www.ldonline_indepth/teaching_techniques/strategies.htm/organization. Teaching organization, active listening, reading, and study skills.

Learning Disabilities Association. (1999). *Speech and language milestones chart* [online]. Retrieved from http://www.ldonline.org/indepth/speech-language/lda-milestones.html

Mid-Continent Research for Education and Learning Lab (http://www.mcrel.org/lesson-plans//lang/index.asp). Language arts lesson plans.

Read, Write, Think (http://www.readwritethink.org). Lesson plans, standards, web resources, and student materials from the International Reading Association, The National Council for Teachers of English, and Marco Polo.

II. Life Skills Resources

Functional Curriculum for Students With Disabilities: Functional Academics (Vol. 3, 3rd ed.), Valletutti, P. V., Bender, M., & Baglin, C.A. (2008). Austin, TX: PRO-ED.

Functional Curriculum for Teaching Students With Disabilities: Nonverbal and Verbal Communication (Vol. 2, 4th ed.), Valletutti, P. V., Bender, M., & Baglin, C. A. (2008). Austin, TX: PRO-ED.

Life Skills Instruction: A Practical Guide for Integrating Real-Life Content Into the Curriculum at the Elementary and Secondary Levels for Students With Special Needs or Who Are Placed at Risk (2nd ed.), Cronin, M. E., Patton, J. R., & Wood, S. J. (2007). Austin, TX: PRO-ED.

Lifelong Learning Skills: How to Teach Today's Children for Tomorrow's Challenges, Lake, J. (1997). Markham, ON, Canada: Pembroke.

Steps to Independence: Teaching Everyday Skills to Children With Special Needs (4th ed.), Baker, B. L., Brightman, A. J., Blacher, J. B., Heifetz, L. J., Hinshaw, S. R., & Murphy, D. M. (2004). Baltimore, MD: Brookes.

III. Instructional Differentiation and Related Inclusion Resources

Accessing the General Curriculum: Including Students With Disabilities in Standards-Based Reform, Nolet, V. & McLaughlin, M. J. (2000). Thousand Oaks, CA: Corwin Press.

Ask for Kids (http://www.askforkids.com). This site has links to various study tools (dictionary, thesaurus, almanac, clip art, science, biography, math help, history), fun and games (classic games, video games, family learning games, and word games), and news resources (e.g., *Weekly Reader, National Geographic for Kids, Kids News Room, BBC for Kids,* and *Scholastic News Zone*).

Differentiated Instructional Strategies: One Size Doesn't Fit All, Gregory, G. H., & Chapman, C. (2002). Thousand Oaks, CA: Corwin Press.

Differentiation in Practice: A Resource Guide for Differentiating Curriculum, Grades 5-9, Tomlinson, C. A. & Cunningham Eidson, C. (2003). Alexandria, VA: Association for Supervision and Curriculum Development.

The Family Involvement Network of Educators (FINE) (http://www.gse.harvard.edu/hfrp/projects/fine.html). Launched by Harvard's Family Research Project, FINE is a national network of more than 2,000 people who are interested in promoting strong partnerships among educators, families, and communities. FINE believes that engaging families is essential to achieving high-performing schools and successful students. The website features monthly announcements, current ideas, new resources, training tools, and a member insight and opinion section.

Kids Click (http://www.kidsclick.org). This website includes links to facts and reference materials, science and math, the environment, several arts sites, health and family, home and household, machines and transportation, society and government, computers and the Internet, and history and biographies. The site also has student-safe and child-friendly search tools.

National Institute for Urban School Improvement (http://urbanschools.org). This website contains resources and publications about ways to promote positive linkages among schools, families, and communities.

National Service-Learning Clearinghouse (NSLC) (http://www.servicelearning.org). NSLC provides a user-friendly site for teachers. It offers several resources on service learning, including the *Community-Based Service-Learning Starter Kit,* available on CD-ROM; links to other sites on service learning; funding resources; lesson plans; conferences; and books and other literature on service learning.

Southwest Educational Laboratory (SEDL) (http://www.sedl.org). SEDL is a nonprofit educational research and development corporation. It creates and provides research-based products and services to improve teaching and learning.

Strategies for Success: Classroom Teaching Techniques for Students With Learning Problems (2nd ed.), Meltzer, L. J., Roditi, B. N., Steinberg, J. L., Biddle, K. R., Tauber, S. E., Caron, K. B., & Kniffin, L. (2006). Austin, TX: PRO-ED.

Teachers.net Lesson Bank (http://www.teachers.net/lessons). This website offers lesson plans searchable by curriculum area. It also provides the opportunity to submit and request plans.

Teaching Students Who Are Exceptional, Diverse, and At-Risk in the General Education Classroom (4th ed.), Vaughn S., Bos, C. S., & Schumm, J. S. (2006). Boston: Allyn & Bacon.

Teaching Study Skills to Students With Learning Problems: A Teacher's Guide for Meeting Diverse Needs (2nd ed.), Hoover, J. J., & Patton, J. R. (2007). Austin, TX: PRO-ED.

Terrific Teaching: 100 Great Teachers Share Their Best Ideas, Pratt, D. (1997). Markham, ON, Canada: Pembroke.

Textbooks and the Students Who Can't Read Them, Ciborowski, J. (1992). Cambridge, MA: Brookline.

IV. Technology for Inclusion Resources

Learning with Technology, Dede, C. (1998). Alexandria, VA: Association for Supervision and Curriculum Development.

The Online Classroom: Teaching With the Internet, Cotton, E. G. (1998). Bloomington, IN: EDINFO Press.

Teaching Every Student in the Digital Age: Universal Design for Learning, Rose, D. H., & Meyer, A. (2002). Alexandria, VA: Association for Supervision and Curriculum Development.

Technology for Inclusion: Meeting the Needs of All Students, Male, M. (2003). Boston: Allyn & Bacon.

300 Incredible Things to Do on The Internet, Leebow, K. (1998). Marietta, GA: VIP Publishing.

Universal Design—Digital Content in the Classroom: Toolkits. Software with universal design for learning (UDL) features; it facilitates individualization of learning materials and experiences for maximum inclusion and teaching effectiveness. Available at http://www.cast.org/teachingeverystudent/toolkits/tk_introduction.cfm?tk_id=41.

ABOUT THE AUTHORS

Howard G. Sanford is an associate professor in the Teacher Education Division at Roberts Wesleyan College in Rochester, New York. For more than 26 years he held a full-time teaching and research appointment as a professor in the Department of Special Education at the State University of New York at Geneseo. Howard's primary teaching and research interests have included instructional methodology for students with mild disabilities, particularly for students with learning disabilities in the curricular areas of language arts, mathematics, science, and social studies. In addition, he has taught a variety of assessment courses and collaborated on the standardization of a number of norm-referenced test instruments. He has been professionally involved in the development of a number of instructional materials and continuing education sessions related to career education opportunities in the field of intellectual disabilities and has taught students with and without disabilities at both the elementary and secondary school levels.

Donald S. Marozas is the MacVittie Professor of Education at the State University of New York at Geneseo, where he has taught for 29 years. He received his EdD from Teachers College, Columbia University. He has received numerous awards for his teaching, including being named Arc National Educator of the Year and receiving the Chancellor's Award for Excellence in Teaching at the state level. He co-authored the text *Issues and Practices in Special Education* and has authored or co-authored numerous articles. He has also taught children with and without disabilities of all ages.

Erin Lane Marozas is a first-grade teacher in the Livonia Central School District, New York, where she has taught for 23 years. She received her master's degree from the State University of New York at Geneseo, where she has taught language arts to incoming freshman in the Educational Opportunity Program/Access Opportunity Program for many years. She has worked with students at all levels from pre-K through Grade 6.

James R. Patton is an independent consultant and adjunct associate professor at the University of Texas at Austin. He has taught students with special needs at the elementary, secondary, and postsecondary levels of schooling. Dr. Patton's primary areas of professional activity are transition assessment and planning, life skills instruction, adults with learning disabilities, science education for students with learning problems, and the accommodation of students with special needs in inclusive settings.